Introduction

Words have a lot of power. Sometimes a ⬚ ⬚⬚⬚ all
the difference.

Our words have the remarkable ability to immediately take root in a child's spirit's rich soil.

What we manifest in our lives is also influenced by what we think. However, it is possible to claim that our words have the most power. Our words serve as a powerful confirmation of our innermost feelings. They confirm how we see others, our life, and ourselves in the eyes of the world. Our words provide a powerful affirmation that allows our thoughts to come to life.

Literature is one of the major domains where creativity can be observed, so you must appreciate these classical writers who spend their life fighting to publish their inspiration.

Purpose of this Book

Nowadays there is little time to reflect because the routine consumes us. You must read this collection of classical quotes of famous writers because they spent their life using their creative thinking.

This is a complete list of quotes from famous writers who are unfortunately not with us. The list has no special order. But certainly one of them can inspire you. Also, there are some quotes from famous philosophers from a recent publication.

We hope this collection Inspire You

Humblepics.com

Jane Austen

Jane Austen was an English novelist known primarily for her six major novels, which interpret, critique and comment upon the British landed gentry at the end of the 18th century. Austen's plots often explore the dependence of women on marriage in the pursuit of favorable social standing and economic security. Born: December 16, 1775, Steventon, United Kingdom. Died: July 18, 1817, Winchester, United Kingdom

---

Woman is fine for her own satisfaction alone. No man will admire her the more, no woman will like her the better for it. Neatness and fashion are enough for the former, and a something of shabbiness or impropriety will be most endearing to the latter.

Happiness in marriage is entirely a matter of chance.

Men have had every advantage of us in telling their own story. Education has been

theirs in so much higher a degree; the pen has been in their hands. I will not allow books to prove anything.

Give a girl an education and introduce her properly into the world, and ten to one but she has the means of settling well, without further expense to anybody.

Selfishness must always be forgiven you know, because there is no hope of a cure.

Friendship is certainly the finest balm for the pangs of disappointed love.

General benevolence, but not general friendship, made a man what he ought to be.

Business, you know, may bring you money, but friendship hardly ever does.

Nobody minds having what is too good for them.

My idea of good company is the company of clever, well-informed people who have a great deal of conversation; that is what I call good company.

A large income is the best recipe for happiness I ever heard of.

There is nothing like staying at home for real comfort.

A man would always wish to give a woman a better home than the one he takes her from; and he who can do it, where there is no doubt of her regard, must, I think, be the happiest of mortals.

Selfishness must always be forgiven you know, because there is no hope of a cure.

A lady's imagination is very rapid; it jumps from admiration to love, from love to matrimony in a moment.

It is a truth universally acknowledged, that a single man in possession of a good fortune, must be in want of a wife.

Happiness in marriage is entirely a matter of chance.

It is always incomprehensible to a man that a woman should ever refuse an offer of marriage.

Men have had every advantage of us in telling their own story. Education has been theirs in so much higher a degree; the pen has been in their hands. I will not allow books to prove anything.

Friendship is certainly the finest balm for the pangs of disappointed love.

To sit in the shade on a fine day and look upon verdure is the most perfect refreshment.

They are much to be pitied who have not been given a taste for nature early in life.

The power of doing anything with quickness is always prized much by the possessor, and often without any attention to the imperfection of the performance.

Respect for right conduct is felt by every body.

There is no charm equal to tenderness of heart.

Charles Dickens

Charles John Huffam Dickens was an English writer and social critic. He created some of the world's best-known fictional characters and is regarded by many as the greatest novelist of the Victorian era. Born: February 7, 1812, Landport, Portsmouth, United Kingdom. Died: June 9, 1870, Gads Hill Place, United Kingdom.

The age of chivalry is past. Bores have succeeded to dragons.

It was the best of times, it was the worst of times.

The first rule of business is: Do other men for they would do you.

That sort of half sigh, which, accompanied by two or three slight nods of the head, is pity's small change in general society.

I will honor Christmas in my heart, and try to keep it all the year.

Christmas time! That man must be a misanthrope indeed, in whose breast something like a jovial feeling is not roused - in whose mind some pleasant associations are not awakened - by the recurrence of Christmas.

Electric communication will never be a substitute for the face of someone who with their soul encourages another person to be brave and true.

I only ask to be free. The butterflies are free.

Fan the sinking flame of hilarity with the wing of friendship; and pass the rosy wine.

Whatever I have tried to do in life, I have tried with all my heart to do it well; whatever I have devoted myself to, I have devoted myself completely; in great aims and in small I have always thoroughly been in earnest.

Great men are seldom over-scrupulous in the arrangement of their attire.

Charity begins at home, and justice begins next door.

Home is a name, a word, it is a strong one; stronger than magician ever spoke, or spirit ever answered to, in the strongest conjuration.

A loving heart is the truest wisdom.

The first rule of business is: Do other men for they would do you.

Reflect upon your present blessings of which every man has many - not on your past misfortunes, of which all men have some.

The men who learn endurance, are they who call the whole world, brother.

The civility which money will purchase, is rarely extended to those who have none.

Nature gives to every time and season some beauties of its own; and from morning to night, as from the cradle to the grave, it is but a succession of changes so gentle and easy that we can scarcely mark their progress.

Nature gives to every time and season some beauties of its own; and from morning to night, as from the cradle to the grave, it is but a succession of changes so gentle and easy that we can scarcely mark their progress.

That sort of half sigh, which, accompanied by two or three slight nods of the head, is pity's small change in general society.

The men who learn endurance, are they who call the whole world, brother.

There are dark shadows on the earth, but its lights are stronger in the contrast.

I never could have done what I have done without the habits of punctuality, order, and diligence, without the determination to concentrate myself on one subject at a time.

I have known a vast quantity of nonsense talked about bad men not looking you in the face. Don't trust that conventional idea. Dishonesty will stare honesty out of countenance any day in the week, if there is anything to be got by it.

Virginia Woolf

Adeline Virginia Woolf was an English writer, considered one of the most important modernist 20th-century authors and a pioneer in the use of stream of consciousness as a narrative device. Born: January 25, 1882, Kensington, London, United Kingdom. Died: March 28, 1941, Lewes, United Kingdom.

It's not catastrophes, murders, deaths, diseases, that age and kill us; it's the way people look and laugh, and run up the steps of omnibuses.

Rigid, the skeleton of habit alone upholds the human frame.

When the shriveled skin of the ordinary is stuffed out with meaning, it satisfies the senses amazingly.

The beauty of the world, which is so soon to perish, has two edges, one of laughter, one of anguish, cutting the heart asunder.

Yet, it is true, poetry is delicious; the best prose is that which is most full of poetry.

Mental fight means thinking against the current, not with it. It is our business to puncture gas bags and discover the seeds of truth.

This soul, or life within us, by no means agrees with the life outside us. If one has the courage to ask her what she thinks, she is always saying the very opposite to what other people say.

Someone has to die in order that the rest of us should value life more.

Yet it is in our idleness, in our dreams, that the submerged truth sometimes comes to the top.

It is in our idleness, in our dreams, that the submerged truth sometimes comes to the top.

One cannot think well, love well, sleep well, if one has not dined well.

To enjoy freedom we have to control ourselves.

Some people go to priests; others to poetry; I to my friends.

For most of history, Anonymous was a woman.

Humor is the first of the gifts to perish in a foreign tongue.

The man who is aware of himself is henceforward independent; and he is never bored, and life is only too short, and he is *steeped through and through with a profound yet temperate happiness.*

There can be no two opinions as to what a highbrow is. He is the man or woman of thoroughbred intelligence who rides his mind at a gallop across country in pursuit of an idea.

A woman must have money and a room of her own if she is to write fiction.

You cannot find peace by avoiding life.

Yet, it is true, poetry is delicious; the best prose is that which is most full of poetry.

Some people go to priests; others to poetry; I to my friends.

The telephone, which interrupts the most serious conversations and cuts short the most weighty observations, has a romance of its own.

Fyodor Dostoevsky

Fyodor Mikhailovich Dostoevsky, sometimes transliterated as Dostoyevsky, was a Russian novelist, short story writer, essayist, and journalist. Born: November 11, 1821, Moscow, Russia. Died: February 9, 1881, Saint Petersburg, Russia.

Beauty is mysterious as well as terrible. God and devil are fighting there, and the battlefield is the heart of man.

Men do not accept their prophets and slay them, but they love their martyrs and worship those whom they have tortured to death.

There are things which a man is afraid to tell even to himself, and every decent man has a number of such things stored away in his mind.

Realists do not fear the results of their study.

Beauty is mysterious as well as terrible. God and devil are fighting there, and the battlefield is the heart of man.

To love someone means to see him as God intended him.

One can know a man from his laugh, and if you like a man's laugh before you know anything of him, you may confidently say that he is a good man.

The greatest happiness is to know the source of unhappiness.

Happiness does not lie in happiness, but in the achievement of it.

The greatest happiness is to know the source of unhappiness.

Man is fond of counting his troubles, but he does not count his joys. If he counted them up as he ought to, he would see that every lot has enough happiness provided for it.

To live without Hope is to Cease to live.

To love someone means to see him as God intended him.

Deprived of meaningful work, men and women lose their reason for existence; they go stark, raving mad.

Men do not accept their prophets and slay them, but they love their martyrs and worship those whom they have tortured to death.

A real gentleman, even if he loses everything he owns, must show no emotion. Money must be so far beneath a gentleman that it is hardly worth troubling about.

A novel is a work of poetry. In order to write it, one must have tranquility of spirit and of impression.

Mark Twain

Samuel Langhorne Clemens, known by his pen name Mark Twain, was an American writer, humorist, entrepreneur, publisher, and lecturer. Born: November 30, 1835, Florida, Missouri, United States. Died: April 21, 1910, Redding, Connecticut, United States.

Age is an issue of mind over matter. If you don't mind, it doesn't matter.

Wrinkles should merely indicate where smiles have been.

Life would be infinitely happier if we could only be born at the age of eighty and gradually approach eighteen.

Lord save us all from old age and broken health and a hope tree that has lost the faculty of putting out blossoms.

Anger is an acid that can do more harm to the vessel in which it is stored than to anything on which it is poured.

When angry, count to four; when very angry, swear.

The best way to cheer yourself up is to try to cheer somebody else up.

If it's your job to eat a frog, it's best to do it first thing in the morning. And If it's your job to eat two frogs, it's best to eat the biggest one first.

Honesty is the best policy - when there is money in it.

We have the best government that money can buy.

It were not best that we should all think alike; it is difference of opinion that makes horse races.

Prosperity is the best protector of principle.

It is better to keep your mouth closed and let people think you are a fool than to open it and remove all doubt.

Whenever you find yourself on the side of the majority, it is time to pause and reflect.

Prophesy is a good line of business, but it is full of risks.

Necessity is the mother of taking chances.

When a person cannot deceive himself the chances are against his being able to deceive other people.

It usually takes me more than three weeks to prepare a good impromptu speech.

Words are only painted fire; a look is the fire itself.

A man's character may be learned from the adjectives which he habitually uses in conversation.

Courage is resistance to fear, mastery of fear, not absence of fear.

It is curious that physical courage should be so common in the world and moral courage so rare.

I didn't attend the funeral, but I sent a nice letter saying I approved of it.

The fear of death follows from the fear of life. A man who lives fully is prepared to die at any time.

Do the thing you fear most and the death of fear is certain.

The reports of my death have been greatly exaggerated.

The only way to keep your health is to eat what you don't want, drink what you don't like, and do what you'd rather not.

A person who won't read has no advantage over one who can't read.

In the first place, God made idiots. That was for practice. Then he made school boards.

Don't let schooling interfere with your education.

Training is everything. The peach was once a bitter almond; cauliflower is nothing but cabbage with a college education.

Cauliflower is nothing but cabbage with a college education.

Education consists mainly of what we have unlearned.

I never let schooling interfere with my education.

Soap and education are not as sudden as a massacre, but they are more deadly in the long run.

A man who carries a cat by the tail learns something he can learn in no other way.

The fear of death follows from the fear of life. A man who lives fully is prepared to die at any time.

Courage is resistance to fear, mastery of fear, not absence of fear.

Do the thing you fear most and the death of fear is certain.

I have never taken any exercise, except sleeping and resting, and I never intend to take any.

Part of the secret of a success in life is to eat what you like and let the food fight it out inside.

Forgiveness is the fragrance that the violet sheds on the heel that has crushed it.

William Shakespeare

William Shakespeare was an English playwright, poet and actor, widely regarded as the greatest writer in the English language and the world's greatest dramatist. He is often called England's national poet and the "Bard of Avon. Born: April 1564, Stratford-upon-Avon, United Kingdom. Died: April 23, 1616, Stratford-upon-Avon, United Kingdom.

A man loves the meat in his youth that he cannot endure in his age.

There's no art to find the mind's construction in the face.

But men are men; the best sometimes forget.

'Tis best to weigh the enemy more mighty than he seems.

Brevity is the soul of wit.

Boldness be my friend.

Good night, good night! Parting is such sweet sorrow, that I shall say good night till it be morrow.

Cowards die many times before their deaths; the valiant never taste of death but once.

Death is a fearful thing.

I were better to be eaten to death with a rust than to be scoured to nothing with perpetual motion.

The stroke of death is as a lover's pinch, which hurts and is desired.

The valiant never taste of death but once.

*We are such stuff as dreams are made on;
and our little life is rounded with a sleep.*

The love of heaven makes one heavenly.

*Now, God be praised, that to believing
souls gives light in darkness, comfort in
despair.*

*Faith, there hath been many great men
that have flattered the people who ne'er
loved them.*

It is a wise father that knows his own child.

*Things done well and with a care, exempt
themselves from fear.*

In time we hate that which we often fear.

If music be the food of love, play on.

Sweet mercy is nobility's true badge.

It is not in the stars to hold our destiny but in ourselves.

God has given you one face, and you make yourself another.

Ignorance is the curse of God; knowledge is the wing wherewith we fly to heaven.

What a piece of work is a man, how noble in reason, how infinite in faculties, in form and moving how express and admirable, in action how like an angel, in apprehension how like a god.

Now, God be praised, that to believing souls gives light in darkness, comfort in despair.

There is nothing either good or bad but thinking makes it so.

How far that little candle throws its beams! So shines a good deed in a naughty world.

Our doubts are traitors and make us lose the good we oft might win by fearing to attempt.

Good night, good night! Parting is such sweet sorrow, that I shall say good night till it be morrow.

The evil that men do lives after them; the good is oft interred with their bones.

Some are born great, some achieve greatness, and some have greatness thrust upon them.

To do a great right do a little wrong.

When we are born we cry that we are come to this great stage of fools.

F. Scott Fitzgerald

Francis Scott Key Fitzgerald was an American novelist, essayist, short story writer and screenwriter. He was best known for his novels depicting the flamboyance and excess of the Jazz Age—a term he popularized. During his lifetime, he published four novels, four story collections, and 164 short stories. Born: September 24, 1896, Saint Paul, Minnesota, United States. Died: December 21, 1940, Hollywood, Los Angeles, California, United States

Nothing is as obnoxious as other people's luck.

Genius is the ability to put into effect what is on your mind.

Family quarrels are bitter things. They don't go according to any rules. They're not

like aches or wounds, they're more like splits in the skin that won't heal because there's not enough material.

Forgotten is forgiven.

A great social success is a pretty girl who plays her cards as carefully as if she were plain.

Life is essentially a cheat and its conditions are those of defeat; the redeeming things are not happiness and pleasure but the deeper satisfactions that come out of struggle.

I'm a romantic; a sentimental person thinks things will last, a romantic person hopes against hope that they won't.

Vitality shows in not only the ability to persist but the ability to start over.

The test of a first-rate intelligence is the ability to hold two opposed ideas in mind at the same time and still retain the ability to function.

It occurred to me that there was no difference between men, in intelligence or race, so profound as the difference between the sick and the well.

Men get to be a mixture of the charming mannerisms of the women they have known.

In a real dark night of the soul, it is always three o'clock in the morning, day after day.

Advertising is a racket, like the movies and the brokerage business. You cannot be honest without admitting that its constructive contribution to humanity is exactly minus zero.

First you take a drink, then the drink takes a drink, then the drink takes you.

For awhile after you quit Keats all other poetry seems to be only whistling or humming.

Either you think, or else others have to think for you and take power from you, pervert and discipline your natural tastes, civilize and sterilize you.

Often people display a curious respect for a man drunk, rather like the respect of simple races for the insane... There is something awe-inspiring in one who has lost all inhibitions.

I'm a romantic; a sentimental person thinks things will last, a romantic person hopes against hope that they won't.

The compensation of a very early success is a conviction that life is a romantic matter. In the best sense one stays young.

It is sadder to find the past again and find it inadequate to the present than it is to have it elude you and remain forever a harmonious conception of memory.

The victor belongs to the spoils.

A great social success is a pretty girl who plays her cards as carefully as if she were plain.

The test of a first-rate intelligence is the ability to hold two opposed ideas in mind at the same time and still retain the ability to function.

Herman Melville

Herman Melville was an American novelist, short story writer, and poet of the American Renaissance period. Among his best-known works are Moby-Dick and Typee. Born: August 1, 1819, New York, New York, United States. Died: September 28, 1891, New York, New York, United States.

Art is the objectification of feeling.

Friendship at first sight, like love at first sight, is said to be the only truth.

There are times when even the most potent governor must wink at transgression, in order to preserve the laws inviolate for the future.

He who has never failed somewhere, that man can not be great.

Hope is the struggle of the soul, breaking loose from what is perishable, and attesting her eternity.

Friendship at first sight, like love at first sight, is said to be the only truth.

We cannot live only for ourselves. A thousand fibers connect us with our fellow men.

At sea a fellow comes out. Salt water is like wine, in that respect.

A smile is the chosen vehicle of all ambiguities.

Let us speak, though we show all our faults and weaknesses, - for it is a sign of strength to be weak, to know it, and out with it - not in a set way and ostentatiously, though, but incidentally and without premeditation.

In this world, shipmates, sin that pays its way can travel freely, and without passport; whereas Virtue, if a pauper, is stopped at all frontiers.

Ernest Hemingway

Ernest Miller Hemingway was an American novelist, short-story writer, journalist, and sportsman. His economical and understated style—which he termed the iceberg theory—had a strong influence on 20th-century fiction, while his adventurous lifestyle and his public image brought him admiration from later generations. Born: July 21, 1899, Oak Park, Illinois, United States. Died: July 2, 1961, Ketchum, Idaho, United States

---

Hesitation increases in relation to risk in equal proportion to age.

You can write any time people will leave you alone and not interrupt you. Or, rather, you can if you will be ruthless enough about it. But the best writing is certainly when you are in love.

Switzerland is a small, steep country, much more up and down than sideways, and is all stuck over with large brown hotels built on the cuckoo clock style of architecture.

Prose is architecture, not interior decoration, and the Baroque is over.

You're beautiful, like a May fly.

The best way to find out if you can trust somebody is to trust them.

My aim is to put down on paper what I see and what I feel in the best and simplest way.

Never mistake motion for action.

It's none of their business that you have to learn how to write. Let them think you were born that way.

I always rewrite each day up to the point where I stopped. When it is all finished, naturally you go over it. You get another chance to correct and rewrite when someone else types it, and you see it clean

*in type. The last chance is in the proofs.
You're grateful for these different chances.*

*I learned never to empty the well of my
writing, but always to stop when there was
still something there in the deep part of the
well, and let it refill at night from the
springs that fed it.*

*When I am working on a book or a story, I
write every morning as soon after first light
as possible. There is no one to disturb you,
and it is cool or cold, and you come to your
work and warm as you write.*

Courage is grace under pressure.

*There is no lonelier man in death, except
the suicide, than that man who has lived
many years with a good wife and then
outlived her. If two people love each other
there can be no happy end to it.*

Madame, all stories, if continued far enough, end in death, and he is no true-story teller who would keep that from you.

Once writing has become your major vice and greatest pleasure, only death can stop it.

Fear of death increases in exact proportion to increase in wealth.

Bullfighting is the only art in which the artist is in danger of death and in which the degree of brilliance in the performance is left to the fighter's honor.

You see, I am trying in all my stories to get the feeling of the actual life across - not to just depict life - or criticize it - but to actually make it alive. So that when you have read something by me, you actually experience the thing. You can't do this without putting in the bad and the ugly as well as what is beautiful.

But man is not made for defeat. A man can be destroyed but not defeated.

Man is not made for defeat.

Fear of death increases in exact proportion to increase in wealth.

A man's got to take a lot of punishment to write a really funny book.

There is no lonelier man in death, except the suicide, than that man who has lived many years with a good wife and then outlived her. If two people love each other there can be no happy end to it.

About morals, I know only that what is moral is what you feel good after and what is immoral is what you feel bad after.

For a true writer, each book should be a new beginning where he tries again for something that is beyond attainment. He should always try for something that has never been done or that others have tried and failed. Then sometimes, with great luck, he will succeed.

I like to listen. I have learned a great deal from listening carefully. Most people never listen.

Happiness in intelligent people is the rarest thing I know.

The only thing that could spoil a day was people. People were always the limiters of happiness except for the very few that were as good as spring itself.

George Orwell

Eric Arthur Blair, known by his pen name George Orwell, was an English novelist, essayist, journalist and critic. His work is characterized by lucid prose, biting social criticism, total opposition to totalitarianism, and outspoken support of democratic socialism. Born: June 25, 1903, Motihari, India. Died: January 21, 1950, University College Hospital, London, United Kingdom

All animals are equal, but some animals are more equal than others.

As with the Christian religion, the worst advertisement for Socialism is its adherents.

Doublethink means the power of holding two contradictory beliefs in one's mind simultaneously, and accepting both of them.

Each generation imagines itself to be more intelligent than the one that went before it, and wiser than the one that comes after it.

Every war when it comes, or before it comes, is represented not as a war but as an act of self-defense against a homicidal maniac.

Freedom is the freedom to say that two plus two make four. If that is granted, all else follows.

Freedom is the right to tell people what they do not want to hear.

Happiness can exist only in acceptance.

I doubt whether classical education ever has been or can be successfully carried out without corporal punishment.

If you want a vision of the future, imagine a boot stamping on a human face - forever.

In our age there is no such thing as 'keeping out of politics.' All issues are political issues, and politics itself is a mass of lies, evasions, folly, hatred and schizophrenia.

Men are only as good as their technical development allows them to be.

Men can only be happy when they do not assume that the object of life is happiness.

Nationalism is power hunger tempered by self-deception.

No advance in wealth, no softening of manners, no reform or revolution has ever brought human equality a millimeter nearer.

Not to expose your true feelings to an adult seems to be instinctive from the age of seven or eight onwards.

Oceania was at war with Eurasia; therefore Oceania had always been at war with Eurasia.

On the whole, human beings want to be good, but not too good, and not quite all the time.

Patriotism is usually stronger than class hatred, and always stronger than internationalism.

People sleep peaceably in their beds at night only because rough men stand ready to do violence on their behalf.

Power is not a means, it is an end. One does not establish a dictatorship in order to safeguard a revolution; one makes the revolution in order to establish the dictatorship.

Serious sport is war minus the shooting.

Society has always to demand a little more from human beings than it will get in practice.

Sometimes the first duty of intelligent men is the restatement of the obvious.

The best books... are those that tell you what you know already.

The essential act of war is destruction, not necessarily of human lives, but of the products of human labor.

The quickest way of ending a war is to lose it.

The very concept of objective truth is fading out of the world. Lies will pass into history.

There are some ideas so wrong that only a very intelligent person could believe in them.

There is hardly such a thing as a war in which it makes no difference who wins. Nearly always one side stands more or less for progress, the other side more or less for reaction.

To walk through the ruined cities of Germany is to feel an actual doubt about the continuity of civilization.

Vladimir Nabokov

Vladimir Vladimirovich Nabokov, also known by the pen name Vladimir Sirin, was a Russian-American novelist, poet, translator, and entomologist. Born in Russia, he wrote his first nine novels in Russian while living in Berlin. Born: April 22, 1899, Saint Petersburg, Russia. Died: July 2, 1977, Montreux, Switzerland.

Complacency is a state of mind that exists only in retrospective: it has to be shattered before being ascertained.

The breaking of a wave cannot explain the whole sea.

I think it is all a matter of love: the more you love a memory, the stronger and stranger it is.

Life is a great sunrise. I do not see why death should not be an even greater one.

The cradle rocks above an abyss, and common sense tells us that our existence is but a brief crack of light between two eternities of darkness.

I think like a genius, I write like a distinguished author, and I speak like a child.

Caress the detail, the divine detail.

The pages are still blank, but there is a miraculous feeling of the words being there, written in invisible ink and clamoring to become visible.

Existence is a series of footnotes to a vast, obscure, unfinished masterpiece.

There is nothing in the world that I loathe more than group activity, that communal bath where the hairy and slippery mix in a multiplication of mediocrity.

Genius is an African who dreams up snow.

Nothing revives the past so completely as a smell that was once associated with it.

Literature and butterflies are the two sweetest passions known to man.

A work of art has no importance whatever to society. It is only important to the individual.

Imagination, the supreme delight of the immortal and the immature, should be limited. In order to enjoy life, we should not enjoy it too much.

Happy is the novelist who manages to preserve an actual love letter that he received when he was young within a work of fiction, embedded in it like a clean bullet in flabby flesh and quite secure there, among spurious lives.

I have often noticed that after I had bestowed on the characters of my novels some treasured item of my past, it would pine away in the artificial world where I had so abruptly placed it.

I confess, I do not believe in time.

A writer should have the precision of a poet and the imagination of a scientist.

Style and Structure are the essence of a book; great ideas are hogwash.

Poetry involves the mysteries of the irrational perceived through rational words.

The evolution of sense is, in a sense, the evolution of nonsense.

It is hard, I submit, to loathe bloodshed, including war, more than I do, but it is still harder to exceed my loathing of the very nature of totalitarian states in which massacre is only an administrative detail.

You can always count on a murderer for a fancy prose style.

The more gifted and talkative one's characters are, the greater the chances of their resembling the author in tone or tint of mind.

Jules Verne

Jules Gabriel Verne was a French novelist, poet, and playwright. His collaboration with the publisher Pierre-Jules Hetzel led to the creation of the "Voyages extraordinaires" a series of bestselling adventure novels including Journey to the Center of the Earth (1864), Twenty Thousand Leagues Under the Seas (1870), and Around the World in Eighty Days (1872). Born: February 8, 1828, Nantes, France
Died: March 24, 1905, Amiens, France.

Put two ships in the open sea, without wind or tide, and, at last, they will come together. Throw two planets into space, and they will fall one on the other. Place two enemies in the midst of a crowd, and they will inevitably meet; it is a fatality, a question of time; that is all.

Science, my lad, is made up of mistakes, but they are mistakes which it is useful to make, because they lead little by little to the truth.

Movement is life;' and it is well to be able to forget the past, and kill the present by continual change.

Solitude, isolation, are painful things and beyond human endurance.

I believe cats to be spirits come to earth. A cat, I am sure, could walk on a cloud without coming through.

We may brave human laws, but we cannot resist natural ones.

When the mind once allows a doubt to gain entrance, the value of deeds performed grow less, their character changes, we forget the past and dread the future.

Nothing can astound an American. It has often been asserted that the word 'impossible' is not a French one. People have evidently been deceived by the *dictionary. In America, all is easy, all is simple; and as for mechanical difficulties, they are overcome before they arise.*

Trains, like time and tide, stop for no one.

Fellows who have rascally faces have only one course to take, and that is to remain honest; otherwise, they would be arrested off-hand.

It is said that the night brings counsel, but it is not said that the counsel is necessarily good.

It is for others one must learn to do everything; for there lies the secret of happiness.

The sea is everything. It covers seven tenths of the terrestrial globe. Its breath is pure and healthy. It is an immense desert, where man is never lonely, for he feels life stirring on all sides.

Ah! Young people, travel if you can, and if you cannot - travel all the same!

Liberty is worth paying for.

In presence of Nature's grand convulsions, man is powerless.

The sea is only the embodiment of a supernatural and wonderful existence.

With happiness as with health: to enjoy it, one should be deprived of it occasionally.

In spite of the opinions of certain narrow-minded people, who would shut up the human race upon this globe, as within some magic circle it must never outstep, we shall one day travel to the moon, the planets, and the stars, with the same facility, rapidity, and certainty as we now make the voyage from Liverpool to New York!

Man is never perfect nor contented.

One has only to follow events, and you will be all right. The surest way is to take whatever comes as it comes.

The sea is the vast reservoir of Nature. The globe began with sea, so to speak; and who knows if it will not end with it?

Imagine a society in which there were neither rich nor poor. What evils, afflictions, sorrows, disorders, catastrophes, disasters, tribulations, misfortunes, agonies, calamities, despair, desolation and ruin would be unknown to man!

The sea does not belong to despots. Upon its surface men can still exercise unjust laws, fight, tear one another to pieces, and be carried away with terrestrial horrors. But at thirty feet below its level, their reign ceases, their influence is quenched, and their power disappears.

Be it understood you are never rich when you get no advantage from it.

How many persons condemned to the horrors of solitary confinement have gone mad - simply because the thinking faculties have lain dormant!

Dante Alighieri

Dante Alighieri, probably baptized Durante di Alighiero degli Alighieri and often referred to simply as Dante, was an Italian poet, writer and philosopher. Born: 1265, Florence, Italy. Died: September 14, 1321, Ravenna, Italy.

The darkest places in hell are reserved for those who maintain their neutrality in times of moral crisis.

Beauty awakens the soul to act.

Consider your origins: you were not made to live as brutes, but to follow virtue and knowledge.

There is no greater sorrow than to recall happiness in times of misery.

Nature is the art of God.

You shall find out how salt is the taste of another man's bread, and how hard is the way up and down another man's stairs.

From a little spark may burst a flame.

Follow your own star!

In the middle of the journey of our life I came to myself within a dark wood where the straight way was lost.

Art, as far as it is able, follows nature, as a pupil imitates his master; thus your art must be, as it were, God's grandchild.

Remember tonight... for it is the beginning of always.

A mighty flame followeth a tiny spark.

Heaven wheels above you, displaying to you her eternal glories, and still your eyes are on the ground.

Be as a tower firmly set; Shakes not its top for any blast that blows.

The secret of getting things done is to act!

Heat cannot be separated from fire, or beauty from The Eternal.

All hope abandon, ye who enter here!

He listens well who takes notes.

I wept not, so to stone within I grew.

Pride, envy, avarice - these are the sparks have set on fire the hearts of all men.

The more perfect a thing is, the more susceptible to good and bad treatment it is.

The sad souls of those who lived without blame and without praise.

I love to doubt as well as know.

Worldly fame is but a breath of wind that blows now this way, and now that, and changes name as it changes direction.

At this high moment, ability failed my capacity to describe.

If the present world go astray, the cause is in you, in you it is to be sought.

Homer

Homer was an ancient Greek author and epic poet. He is the reputed author of the Iliad and the Odyssey, the two epic poems that are the foundational works of ancient Greek literature. Born: Ionia. Died: Ios, Greece.

*Without a sign, his sword the brave man draws,
and asks no omen, but his country's cause.*

Wise to resolve, and patient to perform.

*Yet, taught by time, my heart has learned to glow
for other's good, and melt at other's woe.*

*There is nothing nobler or more admirable than
when two people who see eye to eye keep house
as man and wife, confounding their enemies and
delighting their friends.*

How vain, without the merit, is the name.

*The difficulty is not so great to die for a friend, as
to find a friend worth dying for.*

*Be still my heart; thou hast known worse than
this.*

In youth and beauty, wisdom is but rare!

Light is the task where many share the toil.

Hateful to me as the gates of Hades is that man who hides one thing in his heart and speaks another.

There is a time for many words, and there is also a time for sleep.

Words empty as the wind are best left unsaid.

A sympathetic friend can be quite as dear as a brother.

The charity that is a trifle to us can be precious to others.

Two friends, two bodies with one soul inspired.

A decent boldness ever meets with friends.

And what he greatly thought, he nobly dared.

Hateful to me as are the gates of hell, Is he who, hiding one thing in his heart, Utters another.

It is not good to have a rule of many.

Hunger is insolent, and will be fed.

True friends appear less moved than counterfeit.

To have a great man for an intimate friend seems pleasant to those who have never tried it; those who have, fear it.

Nothing shall I, while sane, compare with a friend.

For rarely are sons similar to their fathers: most are worse, and a few are better than their fathers.

Two urns on Jove's high throne have ever stood, the source of evil one, and one of good; from thence the cup of mortal man he fills, blessings to these, to those distributes ills; to most he mingles both.

But curb thou the high spirit in thy breast, for gentle ways are best, and keep aloof from sharp contentions.

Miguel de Cervantes

Miguel de Cervantes Saavedra was a Spanish writer widely regarded as the greatest writer in the Spanish language and one of the world's pre-eminent novelists. He is best known for his novel Don Quixote, a work often cited as both the first modern novel and one of the pinnacles of world literature. Born: September 29, 1547, Alcala de Henares, Spain. Died: April 22, 1616, Madrid, Spain.

A proverb is a short sentence based on long experience.

Delay always breeds danger; and to protract a great design is often to ruin it.

Fear has many eyes and can see things underground.

For a man to attain to an eminent degree in learning costs him time, watching, hunger, nakedness, dizziness in the head, weakness in the stomach, and other inconveniences.

He who loses wealth loses much; he who loses a friend loses more; but he that loses his courage loses all.

In order to attain the impossible, one must attempt the absurd.

It is one thing to praise discipline, and another to submit to it.

Never stand begging for that which you have the power to earn.

No fathers or mothers think their own children ugly.

One man scorned and covered with scars still strove with his last ounce of courage to reach the unreachable stars; and the world will be better for this.

Proverbs are short sentences drawn from long experience.

The eyes those silent tongues of love.

The knowledge of yourself will preserve you from vanity.

There is also this benefit in brag, that the speaker is unconsciously expressing his own ideal. Humor him by all means, draw it all out, and hold him to it.

To be prepared is half the victory.

To withdraw is not to run away, and to stay is no wise action, when there's more reason to fear than to hope.

Valor lies just halfway between rashness and cowardice.

John Milton

John Milton was an English poet and intellectual who served as a civil servant for the Commonwealth of England under its Council of State and later under Oliver Cromwell. He wrote at a time of religious flux and political upheaval, and is best known for his epic poem Paradise Lost. Born: December 9, 1608, Bread Street, London, United Kingdom
Died: November 8, 1674, Bunhill Row

The mind is its own place and in itself, can make a Heaven of Hell, a Hell of Heaven.

He who reigns within himself and rules passions, desires, and fears is more than a king.

Death is the golden key that opens the palace of eternity.

Give me the liberty to know, to utter, and to argue freely according to conscience, above all liberties.

Gratitude bestows reverence, allowing us to encounter everyday epiphanies, those transcendent moments of awe that change forever how we experience life and the world.

None can love freedom heartily, but good men; the rest love not freedom, but license.

To be blind is not miserable; not to be able to bear blindness, that is miserable.

They also serve who only stand and wait.

Who kills a man kills a reasonable creature, God's image, but thee who destroys a good book, kills reason its self.

The stars, that nature hung in heaven, and filled their lamps with everlasting oil, give due light to the misled and lonely traveler.

For what can war, but endless war, still breed?

Truth never comes into the world but like a bastard, to the ignominy of him that brought her birth.

A good book is the precious lifeblood of a master spirit.

Who overcomes by force, hath overcome but half his foe.

Beauty is nature's brag, and must be shown in courts, at feasts, and high solemnities, where most may wonder at the workmanship.

He that studieth revenge keepeth his own wounds green, which otherwise would heal and do well.

Better to reign in hell than serve in heaven.

Confusion heard his voice, and wild uproar Stood ruled, stood vast infinitude confined; Till at his second bidding darkness fled, Light shone, and order from disorder sprung.

Love-quarrels oft in pleasing concord end.

No man who knows aught, can be so stupid to deny that all men naturally were born free.

He that has light within his own clear breast May sit in the center, and enjoy bright day: But he that hides a dark soul and foul thoughts Benighted walks under the mid-day sun; Himself his own dungeon.

The superior man acquaints himself with many sayings of antiquity and many deeds of the past, in order to strengthen his character thereby.

Let not England forget her precedence of teaching nations how to live.

Nothing profits more than self-esteem, grounded on what is just and right.

True it is that covetousness is rich, modesty starves.

When complaints are freely heard, deeply considered and speedily reformed, then is the utmost bound of civil liberty attained that wise men look for.

Virgil (Virgilio)

Publius Vergilius Maro, usually called Virgil or Vergil in English, was an ancient Roman poet of the Augustan period. He composed three of the most famous poems in Latin literature: the Eclogues, the Georgics, and the epic Aeneid. Born: October 15, 70 BC, Cisalpine Gaul. Died: September 21, 19 BC, Brindisi, Italy.

Come what may, all bad fortune is to be conquered by endurance.

Time flies never to be recalled.

Fortune favours the bold.

It is easy to go down into Hell; night and day, the gates of dark Death stand wide; but to climb back again, to retrace one's steps to the upper air - there's the rub, the task.

They can because they think they can.

It never troubles the wolf how many the sheep may be.

But meanwhile time flies; it flies never to be regained.

Time is flying never to return.

Fate will find a way.

Fortune sides with him who dares.

Fear is proof of a degenerate mind.

They can conquer who believe they can.

They succeed, because they think they can.

Love conquers all.

There's a snake lurking in the grass.

Hug the shore; let others try the deep.

Perhaps even these things, one day, will be pleasing to remember.

O accursed hunger of gold, to what dost thou not compel human hearts!

Consider what each soil will bear, and what each refuses.

Trust not too much to appearances.

Every calamity is to be overcome by endurance.

Even virtue is fairer when it appears in a beautiful person.

Do not yield to misfortunes, but advance more boldly to meet them, as your fortune permits you.

Time passes irrevocably.

Go forth a conqueror and win great victories.

A fault is fostered by concealment.

Geoffrey Chaucer

Geoffrey Chaucer was an English poet, author, and civil servant best known for The Canterbury Tales. He has been called the "father of English literature", or, alternatively, the "father of English poetry". He was the first writer to be buried in what has since come to be called Poets' Corner, in Westminster Abbey. Born: London, United Kingdom. Died: October 25, 1400, London, United Kingdom.

Love is blind.

Time and tide wait for no man.

By nature, men love newfangledness.

People can die of mere imagination.

Murder will out, this my conclusion.

He was as fresh as is the month of May.

And she was fair as is the rose in May.

There's never a new fashion but it's old.

First he wrought, and afterward he taught.

The guilty think all talk is of themselves.

Forbid us something, and that thing we desire.

We know little of the things for which we pray.

The life so short, the crafts so long to learn.

The greatest scholars are not usually the wisest people.

Nowhere so busy a man as he than he, and yet he seemed busier than he was.

There's no workman, whatsoever he be, That may both work well and hastily.

Filth and old age, I'm sure you will agree, are powerful wardens upon chastity.

Whoso will pray, he must fast and be clean, And fat his soul, and make his body lean.

Women desire six things: They want their husbands to be brave, wise, rich, generous, obedient to wife, and lively in bed.

Sophocles

Sophocles is one of three ancient Greek tragedians whose plays have survived. His first plays were written later than, or contemporary with, those of Aeschylus; and earlier than, or contemporary with, those of Euripides. Born: Colonus, Athens, Greece. Died: Classical Athens.

A man growing old becomes a child again.

A word does not frighten the man who, in acting, feels no fear.

Always desire to learn something useful.

Best to live lightly, unthinkingly.

Children are the anchors that hold a mother to life.

For the wretched one night is like a thousand; for someone faring well death is just one more night.

God's dice always have a lucky roll.

Hide nothing, for time, which sees all and hears all, exposes all.

How dreadful knowledge of the truth can be when there's no help in the truth.

Money is the worst currency that ever grew among mankind. This sacks cities, this drives men from their homes, this teaches and corrupts the worthiest minds to turn base deeds.

Old age and the passage of time teach all things.

Our happiness depends on wisdom all the way.

Profit is sweet, even if it comes from deception.

Reason is God's crowning gift to man.

Success is dependent on effort.

The keenest sorrow is to recognize ourselves as the sole cause of all our adversities.

The rewards of virtue alone abide secure.

There is no success without hardship.

Time alone reveals the just man; but you might discern a bad man in a single day.

To him who is in fear everything rustles.

Trust dies but mistrust blossoms.

War never takes a wicked man by chance, the good man always.

When a man has lost all happiness, he's not alive. Call him a breathing corpse.

Who seeks shall find.

Wisdom is the supreme part of happiness.

Wise thinkers prevail everywhere.

You win the victory when you yield to friends.

J. D. Salinger

Jerome David Salinger was an American writer best known for his 1951 novel The Catcher in the Rye. Before its publication, Salinger published several short stories in Story magazine and served in World War II. Born: January 1, 1919, Manhattan, New York, United States. Died: January 27, 2010, Cornish, New Hampshire, United States.

I am a kind of paranoid in reverse. I suspect people of plotting to make me happy.

If a girl looks swell when she meets you, who gives a damn if she's late? Nobody.

How do you know you're going to do something, until you do it?

Mothers are all slightly insane.

I'm sick of just liking people. I wish to God I could meet somebody I could respect.

I'm sick of not having the courage to be an absolute nobody.

I was about half in love with her by the time we sat down. That's the thing about girls. Every time they do something pretty... you fall half in love with them, and then you never know where the hell you are.

How long should a man's legs be? Long enough to touch the ground.

An artist's only concern is to shoot for some kind of perfection, and on his own terms, not anyone else's.

All morons hate it when you call them a moron.

I'm the most terrific liar you ever saw in your life.

Its really hard to be roommates with people if your suitcases are much better than theirs.

I don't exactly know what I mean by that, but I mean it.

Poets are always taking the weather so personally. They're always sticking their emotions in things that have no emotions.

Goddam money. It always ends up making you blue as hell.

The worst thing that being an artist could do to you would be that it would make you slightly unhappy constantly.

I like to write. I love to write. But I write just for myself and my own pleasure.

It was a very stupid thing to do, I'll admit, but I hardly didn't even know I was doing it.

It's funny. All you have to do is say something nobody understands and they'll do practically anything you want them to.

I don't even like old cars. I'd rather have a goddam horse. A horse is at least human, for God's sake.

I'm aware that many of my friends will be saddened and shocked, or shock-saddened, over some of the chapters in 'The Catcher in the Rye.' Some of my best friends are children. In fact, all my best friends are children. It's almost unbearable for me to realize that my book will be kept on a shelf, out of their reach.

People never notice anything.

I'm quite illiterate, but I read a lot.

Some stories, my property, have been stolen. Someone's appropriated them. It's an illicit act. It's unfair. Suppose you had a coat you liked, and somebody went into your closet and stole it. That's how I feel.

You take somebody that cries their goddam eyes out over phony stuff in the movies, and nine times out of ten they're mean bastards at heart.

There is a marvelous peace in not publishing. It's peaceful. Still. Publishing is a terrible invasion of my privacy.

Charlotte Brontë

Charlotte Brontë was an English novelist and poet, the eldest of the three Brontë sisters who survived into adulthood and whose novels became classics of English literature. Born: April 21, 1816, Thornton, United Kingdom. Died: March 31, 1855, Haworth, United Kingdom.

Prejudices, it is well known, are most difficult to eradicate from the heart whose soil has never been loosened or fertilized by education; they grow firm there, firm as weeds among stones.

Life is so constructed, that the event does not, cannot, will not, match the expectation.

The human heart has hidden treasures, In secret kept, in silence sealed; The thoughts, the hopes, the dreams, the pleasures, Whose charms were broken if revealed.

I try to avoid looking forward or backward, and try to keep looking upward.

A ruffled mind makes a restless pillow.

Look twice before you leap.

I am no bird; and no net ensnares me; I am a free human being with an independent will.

Give him enough rope and he will hang himself.

Life appears to me too short to be spent in nursing animosity, or registering wrongs.

Better to be without logic than without feeling.

I feel monotony and death to be almost the same.

If all the world hated you, and believed you wicked, while your own conscience approved you, and absolved you from guilt, you would not be without friends.

If I could I would always work in silence and obscurity, and let my efforts be known by their results.

You know full well as I do the value of sisters' affections: There is nothing like it in this world.

Let your performance do the thinking.

If we would build on a sure foundation in friendship, we must love friends for their sake rather than for our own.

It is in vain to say human beings ought to be satisfied with tranquility: they must have action; and they will make it if they cannot find it.

Men judge us by the success of our efforts. God looks at the efforts themselves.

It is vain to say human beings ought to be satisfied with tranquility; they must have action; and they will make it if they cannot find it.

Cheerfulness, it would appear, is a matter which depends fully as much on the state of things within, as on the state of things without and around us.

Who has words at the right moment?

There is only one difference between a madman and me. I am not mad.

I'm just going to write because I cannot help it.

Consistency, madam, is the first of Christian duties.

If you are cast in a different mould to the majority, it is no merit of yours: Nature did it.

The soul, fortunately, has an interpreter - often an unconscious, but still a truthful interpreter - in the eye.

John Donne

John Donne was an English poet, scholar, soldier and secretary born into a recusant family, who later became a cleric in the Church of England. Under royal patronage, he was made Dean of St Paul's Cathedral in London. He is considered the preeminent representative of the metaphysical poets. Born: January 22, 1572, London, United Kingdom. Died: March 31, 1631, London, United Kingdom.

Any man's death diminishes me, because I am involved in Mankind; And therefore never send to know for whom the bell tolls; it tolls for thee.

For God's sake hold your tongue, and let me love.

No man is an island, entire of itself; every man is a piece of the continent.

Be thine own palace, or the world's thy jail.

Death be not proud, though some have called thee Mighty and dreadful, for thou art not so. For, those, whom thou think'st thou dost overthrow. Die not, poor death, nor yet canst thou kill me.

Nature's great masterpiece, an elephant; the only harmless great thing.

More than kisses, letters mingle souls.

Love, all alike, no season knows, nor clime, nor hours, days, months, which are the rags of time.

And new Philosophy calls all in doubt, the element of fire is quite put out; the Sun is lost, and the earth, and no mans wit can well direct him where to look for it.

Love built on beauty, soon as beauty, dies.

When one man dies, one chapter is not torn out of the book, but translated into a better language.

No spring nor summer beauty hath such grace as I have seen in one autumnal face.

Affliction is a treasure, and scarce any man hath enough of it.

God employs several translators; some pieces are translated by age, some by sickness, some by war, some by justice.

Humiliation is the beginning of sanctification.

As virtuous men pass mildly away, and whisper to their souls to go, whilst some of their sad friends do say, the breath goes now, and some say no.

But I do nothing upon myself, and yet I am my own executioner.

I am two fools, I know, for loving, and for saying so in whining poetry.

Despair is the damp of hell, as joy is the serenity of heaven.

But let them sleep, Lord, and me mourn a space.

Art is the most passionate orgy within man's grasp.

Since you would save none of me, I bury some of you.

He must pull out his own eyes, and see no creature, before he can say, he sees no God; He must be no man, and quench his reasonable soul, before he can say to himself, there is no God.

Pleasure is none, if not diversified.

I observe the physician with the same diligence as the disease.

Reason is our soul's left hand, faith her right.

François Rabelais

François Rabelais was a French Renaissance writer, physician, Renaissance humanist, monk and Greek scholar. He is primarily known as a writer of satire, of the grotesque, and of bawdy jokes and songs. Born: Chinon, France. Died: 1553, Paris, France.

Gestures, in love, are incomparably more attractive, effective and valuable than words.

It is my feeling that Time ripens all things; with Time all things are revealed; Time is the father of truth.

To good and true love fear is forever affixed.

Tell the truth and shame the devil.

Science without conscience is the death of the soul.

We always long for the forbidden things, and desire what is denied us.

When I drink, I think; and when I think, I drink.

Half the world does not know how the other half lives.

Frugality is for the vulgar.

Everything comes in time to those who can wait.

No clock is more regular than the belly.

Debts and lies are generally mixed together.

If you wish to avoid seeing a fool you must first break your looking glass.

The farce is finished. I go to seek a vast perhaps.

A habit does not a monk make.

I have known many who could not when they would, for they had not done it when they could.

If the skies fall, one may hope to catch larks.

The scent of wine, oh how much more agreeable, laughing, praying, celestial and delicious it is than that of oil!

Nature abhors a vacuum.

There are more old drunkards than old physicians.

Ignorance is the mother of all evils.

From the gut comes the strut, and where hunger reigns, strength abstains.

Misery is the company of lawsuits.

The right moment wears a full head of hair: when it has been missed, you can't get it back; it's bald in the back of the head and never turns around.

In their rules there was only one clause: Do what you will.

A bellyful is a bellyful.

William Blake

William Blake was an English poet, painter, and printmaker. Largely unrecognized during his life, Blake is now considered a seminal figure in the history of the poetry and visual art of the Romantic Age. Born: November 28, 1757, Soho, London, United Kingdom. Died: August 12, 1827, London, United Kingdom.

Art can never exist without naked beauty displayed.

Art is the tree of life. Science is the tree of death.

Excessive sorrow laughs. Excessive joy weeps.

Exuberance is beauty.

Fun I love, but too much fun is of all things the most loathsome. Mirth is better than fun, and happiness is better than mirth.

Great things are done when men and mountains meet.

I am in you and you in me, mutual in divine love.

I must create a system or be enslaved by another mans; I will not reason and compare: my business is to create.

If the doors of perception were cleansed everything would appear to man as it is, infinite.

If the Sun and Moon should ever doubt, they'd immediately go out.

Imagination is the real and eternal world of which this vegetable universe is but a faint shadow.

In seed time learn, in harvest teach, in winter enjoy.

It is easier to forgive an enemy than to forgive a friend.

Love seeketh not itself to please, nor for itself hath any care, but for another gives its ease, and builds a Heaven in Hell's despair.

Man has no Body distinct from his Soul; for that called Body is a portion of Soul discerned by the five Senses, the chief inlets of Soul in this age.

No bird soars too high if he soars with his own wings.

One thought fills immensity.

Opposition is true friendship.

*Poetry fettered, fetters the human race.
Nations are destroyed or flourish in
proportion as their poetry, painting, and
music are destroyed or flourish.*

*Prisons are built with stones of Law.
Brothels with the bricks of religion.*

*The bird a nest, the spider a web, man
friendship.*

*The foundation of empire is art and
science. Remove them or degrade them,
and the empire is no more. Empire follows
art and not vice versa as Englishmen
suppose.*

*The glory of Christianity is to conquer by
forgiveness.*

The thankful receiver bears a plentiful harvest.

The true method of knowledge is experiment.

The weak in courage is strong in cunning. Think in the morning. Act in the noon. Eat in the evening. Sleep in the night.

To see a world in a grain of sand and heaven in a wild flower Hold infinity in the palm of your hand and eternity in an hour.

To the eyes of a miser a guinea is more beautiful than the sun, and a bag worn with the use of money has more beautiful proportions than a vine filled with grapes.

Travelers repose and dream among my leaves.

What is grand is necessarily obscure to weak men. That which can be made explicit to the idiot is not worth my care.

What is now proved was once only imagined.

Where mercy, love, and pity dwell, there God is dwelling too.

Voltaire

François-Marie Arouet, known by his nom de plume Voltaire, was a French Enlightenment writer, historian, and philosopher famous for his wit, his criticism of Christianity—especially the Roman Catholic Church—as well as his advocacy of freedom of speech, freedom of religion, and separation of church and state. Born: November 21, 1694, Paris, France. Died: May 30, 1778, Paris, France.

All men are born with a nose and five fingers, but no one is born with a knowledge of God.

All the reasonings of men are not worth one sentiment of women.

Better is the enemy of good.

Chance is a word void of sense; nothing can exist without a cause.

Common sense is not so common.

Divorce is probably of nearly the same date as marriage. I believe, however, that marriage is some weeks the more ancient.

Each player must accept the cards life deals him or her: but once they are in hand, he or she alone must decide how to play the cards in order to win the game.

Every man is guilty of all the good he did not do.

Faith consists in believing when it is beyond the power of reason to believe.

Fear follows crime and is its punishment.

Friendship is the marriage of the soul, and this marriage is liable to divorce.

God gave us the gift of life; it is up to us to give ourselves the gift of living well.

He is a hard man who is only just, and a sad one who is only wise.

He who has not the spirit of this age, has all the misery of it.

He who is not just is severe, he who is not wise is sad.

History is only the register of crimes and misfortunes.

History should be written as philosophy.

I die adoring God, loving my friends, not hating my enemies, and detesting superstition.

I have never made but one prayer to God, a very short one: 'O Lord make my enemies ridiculous.' And God granted it.

If God did not exist, it would be necessary to invent Him.

In general, the art of government consists of taking as much money as possible from one class of citizens to give to another.

Indeed, history is nothing more than a tableau of crimes and misfortunes.

Injustice in the end produces independence.

It is better to risk saving a guilty man than to condemn an innocent one.

It is difficult to free fools from the chains they revere.

It is forbidden to kill; therefore all murderers are punished unless they kill in large numbers and to the sound of trumpets.

It is lamentable, that to be a good patriot one must become the enemy of the rest of mankind.

It is not sufficient to see and to know the beauty of a work. We must feel and be affected by it.

It is said that the present is pregnant with the future.

It is vain for the coward to flee; death follows close behind; it is only by defying it that the brave escape.

Judge a man by his questions rather than his answers.

Life is thickly sown with thorns, and I know no other remedy than to pass quickly through them. The longer we dwell on our misfortunes, the greater is their power to harm us.

Love is a canvas furnished by nature and embroidered by imagination.

Man is free at the moment he wishes to be.

Men use thought only as authority for their injustice, and employ speech only to conceal their thoughts.

Nature has always had more force than education.

Of all religions, the Christian should of course inspire the most tolerance, but until now Christians have been the most intolerant of all men.

One merit of poetry few persons will deny: it says more and in fewer words than prose.

Religion was instituted to make us happy in this life and in the other. What must we do to be happy in the life to come? Be just.

Society therefore is as ancient as the world.

Superstition is to religion what astrology is to astronomy the mad daughter of a wise mother. These daughters have too long dominated the earth.

Tears are the silent language of grief.

The ancient Romans built their greatest masterpieces of architecture, their amphitheaters, for wild beasts to fight in.

The art of medicine consists in amusing the patient while nature cures the disease.

The best government is a benevolent tyranny tempered by an occasional assassination.

The best is the enemy of the good.

The ear is the avenue to the heart.

The instruction we find in books is like fire. We fetch it from our neighbors, kindle it at home, communicate it to others, and it becomes the property of all.

The safest course is to do nothing against one's conscience. With this secret, we can enjoy life and have no fear from death.

The superfluous, a very necessary thing.

The truths of religion are never so well understood as by those who have lost the power of reason.

Gustave Flaubert

Gustave Flaubert was a French novelist. Highly influential, he has been considered the leading exponent of literary realism in his country. Born: December 12, 1821, Rouen, France. Died: May 8, 1880, Croisset, Canteleu, France.

A friend who dies, it's something of you who dies.

All one's inventions are true, you can be sure of that. Poetry is as exact a science as geometry.

Artists who seek perfection in everything are those who cannot attain it in anything.

Everything one invents is true, you may be perfectly sure of that. Poetry is as precise as geometry.

Happiness is a monstrosity! Punished are those who seek it.

I believe that if one always looked at the skies, one would end up with wings.

Life must be a constant education; one must learn everything, from speaking to dying.

Love is a springtime plant that perfumes everything with its hope, even the ruins to which it clings.

Of all lies, art is the least untrue.

Oh, if I had been loved at the age of seventeen, what an idiot I would be today. Happiness is like smallpox: if you catch it too soon, it can completely ruin your constitution.

One can be the master of what one does, but never of what one feels.

One mustn't ask apple trees for oranges, France for sun, women for love, life for happiness.

Poetry is as precise a thing as geometry.

Read in order to live.

The art of writing is the art of discovering what you believe.

The heart, like the stomach, wants a varied diet.

To be stupid, selfish, and have good health are three requirements for happiness, though if stupidity is lacking, all is lost.

Aldous Huxley

Aldous Leonard Huxley was an English writer and philosopher. He wrote nearly 50 books—both novels and non-fiction works—as well as wide-ranging essays, narratives, and poems. Born into the prominent Huxley family, he graduated from Balliol College, Oxford, with an undergraduate degree in English literature. Born: July 26, 1894, Godalming, United Kingdom. Died: November 22, 1963, Los Angeles County, California, United States.

A man may be a pessimistic determinist before lunch and an optimistic believer in the will's freedom after it.

After silence, that which comes nearest to expressing the inexpressible is music.

Beauty is worse than wine, it intoxicates both the holder and beholder.

Children are remarkable for their intelligence and ardor, for their curiosity, their intolerance of shams, the clarity and ruthlessness of their vision.

Consistency is contrary to nature, contrary to life. The only completely consistent people are dead.

Dream in a pragmatic way.

Every man who knows how to read has it in his power to magnify himself, to multiply the ways in which he exists, to make his life full, significant and interesting.

Everyone who wants to do good to the human race always ends in universal bullying.

Experience is not what happens to you; it's what you do with what happens to you.

Experience teaches only the teachable.

From their experience or from the recorded experience of others (history), men learn only what their passions and their metaphysical prejudices allow them to learn.

God isn't compatible with machinery and scientific medicine and universal happiness. You must make your choice. Our civilization has chosen machinery and medicine and happiness.

Happiness is a hard master, particularly other people's happiness.

Like every other good thing in this world, leisure and culture have to be paid for. Fortunately, however, it is not the leisured and the cultured who have to pay.

Man is an intelligence in servitude to his organs.

Men do not learn much from the lessons of history and that is the most important of all the lessons of history.

My father considered a walk among the mountains as the equivalent of churchgoing.

Sons have always a rebellious wish to be disillusioned by that which charmed their fathers.

Specialized meaninglessness has come to be regarded, in certain circles, as a kind of hallmark of true science.

Technological progress has merely provided us with more efficient means for going backwards.

That men do not learn very much from the lessons of history is the most important of all the lessons of history.

The more powerful and original a mind, the more it will incline towards the religion of solitude.

The most valuable of all education is the ability to make yourself do the thing you have to do, when it has to be done, whether you like it or not.

The secret of genius is to carry the spirit of the child into old age, which means never losing your enthusiasm.

The worst enemy of life, freedom and the common decencies is total anarchy; their second worst enemy is total efficiency.

There are things known and there are things unknown, and in between are the doors of perception.

There is only one corner of the universe you can be certain of improving, and that's your own self.

There is something curiously boring about somebody else's happiness.

There isn't any formula or method. You learn to love by loving - by paying attention and doing what one thereby discovers has to be done.

There's only one effectively redemptive sacrifice, the sacrifice of self-will to make room for the knowledge of God.

Thought must be divided against itself before it can come to any knowledge of itself.

To his dog, every man is Napoleon; hence the constant popularity of dogs.

To travel is to discover that everyone is wrong about other countries.

What is absurd and monstrous about war
is that men who have no personal quarrel
should be trained to murder one another in
cold blood.

John Bunyan

John Bunyan was an English writer and Puritan preacher best remembered as the author of the Christian allegory The Pilgrim's Progress, which also became an influential literary model. In addition to The Pilgrim's Progress, Bunyan wrote nearly sixty titles, many of them expanded sermons. Born: 1628, Elstow, United Kingdom. Died: August 31, 1688, Snow Hill, London, United Kingdom.

One leak will sink a ship: and one sin will
destroy a sinner.

My sword I give to him that shall succeed
me in my pilgrimage, and my courage and
skill to him that can get it.

When you pray, rather let your heart be without words than your words without heart.

If we have not quiet in our minds, outward comfort will do no more for us than a golden slipper on a gouty foot.

In prayer it is better to have a heart without words than words without a heart.

He who bestows his goods upon the poor shall have as much again, and ten times more.

There was a castle called Doubting Castle, the owner whereof was Giant Despair.

Words easy to be understood do often hit the mark; when high and learned ones do only pierce the air.

John Steinbeck

John Ernst Steinbeck Jr. was an American author and the 1962 Nobel Prize in Literature winner "for his realistic and imaginative writings, combining as they do sympathetic humor and keen social perception." He has been called "a giant of American letters." Born: February 27, 1902, Salinas, California, United States. Died: December 20, 1968, New York, New York, United States.

*Power does not corrupt. Fear corrupts...
perhaps the fear of a loss of power.*

A sad soul can kill quicker than a germ.

*If you're in trouble or hurt or need - go to
the poor people. They're the only ones
that'll help - the only ones.*

*It is a common experience that a problem
difficult at night is resolved in the morning
after the committee of sleep has worked
on it.*

*A journey is a person in itself; no two are
alike. And all plans, safeguards, policing,
and coercion are fruitless. We find that
after years of struggle that we do not take
a trip; a trip takes us.*

*Ideas are like rabbits. You get a couple and
learn how to handle them, and pretty soon
you have a dozen.*

The discipline of the written word punishes both stupidity and dishonesty.

No one wants advice - only corroboration.

It has always been my private conviction that any man who puts his intelligence up against a fish and loses had it coming.

A journey is like marriage. The certain way to be wrong is to think you control it.

I am impelled, not to squeak like a grateful and apologetic mouse, but to roar like a lion out of pride in my profession.

Man is the only kind of varmint sets his own trap, baits it, then steps in it.

Men do change, and change comes like a little wind that ruffles the curtains at dawn, and it comes like the stealthy perfume of wildflowers hidden in the grass.

I've seen a look in dogs' eyes, a quickly vanishing look of amazed contempt, and I am convinced that basically dogs think humans are nuts.

You know how advice is. You only want it if it agrees with what you wanted to do anyway.

I've lived in good climate, and it bores the hell out of me. I like weather rather than climate.

Many a trip continues long after movement in time and space have ceased.

It seems to me that if you or I must choose between two courses of thought or action, we should remember our dying and try so to live that our death brings no pleasure on the world.

Unless a reviewer has the courage to give you unqualified praise, I say ignore the bastard.

We spend our time searching for security and hate it when we get it.

One can find so many pains when the rain is falling.

In utter loneliness a writer tries to explain the inexplicable.

Man, unlike anything organic or inorganic in the universe, grows beyond his work, walks up the stairs of his concepts, emerges ahead of his accomplishments.

Time is the only critic without ambition.

So in our pride we ordered for breakfast an omelet, toast and coffee and what has just arrived is a tomato salad with onions, a

dish of pickles, a big slice of watermelon
and two bottles of cream soda.

Katherine Mansfield

Kathleen Mansfield Murry was a New Zealand writer, essayist and journalist, widely considered one of the most influential and important authors of the modernist movement. Her works are celebrated across the world and have been published in 25 languages. Born: October 14, 1888, Wellington, New Zealand Died: January 9, 1923, Fontainebleau, France.

Risk! Risk anything! Care no more for the opinions of others, for those voices. Do the hardest thing on earth for you. Act for yourself. Face the truth.

Make it a rule of life never to regret and never to look back. Regret is an appalling waste of energy, you can't build on it it's only good for wallowing in.

This is not a letter but my arms around you for a brief moment.

Everything in life that we really accept undergoes a change.

Life never becomes a habit to me. It's always a marvel.

If only one could tell true love from false love as one can tell mushrooms from toadstools.

I want to be all that I am capable of becoming.

I always felt that the great high privilege, relief and comfort of friendship was that one had to explain nothing.

I want, by understanding myself, to understand others. I want to be all that I am capable of becoming.

Whenever I prepare for a journey I prepare as though for death. Should I never return, all is in order.

Could we change our attitude, we should not only see life differently, but life itself would come to be different.

Some couples go over their budgets very carefully every month. Others just go over them.

Would you not like to try all sorts of lives - one is so very small - but that is the satisfaction of writing - one can impersonate so many people.

It's a terrible thing to be alone - yes it is - it is - but don't lower your mask until you have another mask prepared beneath - as terrible as you like - but a mask.

I love the rain. I want the feeling of it on my face.

Looking back, I imagine I was always writing. Twaddle it was too. But better far write twaddle or anything, anything, than nothing at all.

What do you want most to do? That's what I have to keep asking myself, in the face of difficulties.

Once we have learned to read, meaning of words can somehow register without consciousness.

It is of immense importance to learn to laugh at ourselves.

The pleasure of all reading is doubled when one lives with another who shares the same books.

When we can begin to take our failures seriously, it means we are ceasing to be afraid of them. It is of immense importance to learn to laugh at ourselves.

Elizabeth Bishop

Elizabeth Bishop was an American poet and short-story writer. She was Consultant in Poetry to the Library of Congress from 1949 to 1950, the Pulitzer Prize winner for Poetry in 1956, the National Book Award winner in 1970, and the recipient of the Neustadt International Prize for Literature in 1976. Born: February 8, 1911, Worcester, Massachusetts, United States. Died: October 6, 1979, Lewis Wharf.

The pigs stuck out their little feet and snored.

The whole shadow of Man is only as big as his hat.

The armored cars of dreams, contrived to let us do so many a dangerous thing.

The art of losing isn't hard to master; so many things seem filled with the intent to be lost that their loss is no disaster.

What childishness is it that while there's breath of life in our bodies, we are determined to rush to see the sun the other way around?

All my life I have lived and behaved very much like the sandpiper - just running down the edges of different countries and continents, 'looking for something'.

Dorothy Parker

Dorothy Parker was an American poet, writer, critic, and satirist based in New York; she was best known for her wit, wisecracks, and eye for 20th-century urban foibles. Born: August 22, 1893, Long Branch, New Jersey, United States. Died: June 7, 1967, New York, New York, United States.

Of course I talk to myself. I like a good speaker, and I appreciate an intelligent audience.

Time may be a great healer, but it's a lousy beautician.

If you want to know what God thinks about money, just look at the people He gives it to.

I like to have a martini/Two at the very most/After three I'm under the table/After four I'm under my host.

Never throw mud: you can miss the target,
but your hands will remain dirty.

Creativity is a wild mind and a disciplined
eye.

The cure for boredom is curiosity. There is
no cure for curiosity.

If you don't have anything nice to say,
come sit by me.

If you have any young friends who aspire
to become writers, the second-greatest
favor you can do them is to present them
with copies of The Elements of Style. The
first-greatest, of course, is to shoot them
now, while they're happy.

The first thing I do in the morning is brush
my teeth and sharpen my tongue.

*The only dependable law of life -
everything is always worse than you
thought it was going to be.*

If love is blind, why is lingerie so popular?

*You can lead a horticulture, but you can't
make her think.*

*Years are only garments, and you either
wear them with style all your life, or else
you go dowdy to the grave.*

You can't teach an old dogma new tricks.

Don't look at me in that tone of voice.

Laughter and hope and a sock in the eye.

A hangover is the wrath of grapes.

*I'm not a writer with a drinking problem,
I'm a drinker with a writing problem.*

*Honesty means nothing until you are
tested under circumstances where you are
sure you could get away with dishonesty.*

*Genius can write on the back of old
envelopes but mere talent requires the
finest stationery available.*

*Ducking for apples -- change one letter and
it's the story of my life.*

*This is not a novel to be tossed aside
lightly. It should be thrown with great
force.*

*That would be a good thing for them to cut
on my tombstone: Wherever she went,
including here, it was against her better
judgment.*

Mary Shelley

Mary Wollstonecraft Shelley was an English novelist who wrote the Gothic novel Frankenstein; or, The Modern Prometheus, which is considered an early example of science fiction. She also edited and promoted the works of her husband, the Romantic poet and philosopher Percy Bysshe Shelley. Born: August 30, 1797, Somers Town, London, United Kingdom. Died: February 1, 1851, Chester Square, London, United Kingdom.

And now, once again, I bid my hideous progeny go forth and prosper. I have an affection for it, for it was the offspring of happy days, when death and grief were but words, which found no true echo in my heart.

Nothing contributes so much to tranquilize the mind as a steady purpose - a point on which the soul may fix its intellectual eye.

I do not wish women to have power over men; but over themselves.

My dreams were all my own; I accounted for them to nobody; they were my refuge when annoyed - my dearest pleasure when free.

Invention, it must be humbly admitted, does not consist in creating out of void, but out of chaos.

Life and death appeared to me ideal bounds, which I should first break through, and pour a torrent of light into our dark world.

But I am a blasted tree; the bolt has entered my soul; and I felt then that I should survive to exhibit what I shall soon cease to be - a miserable spectacle of wrecked humanity, pitiable to others and intolerable to myself.

The very winds whispered in soothing accents, and maternal Nature bade me weep no more.

The agony of my feelings allowed me no respite; no incident occurred from which my rage and misery could not extract its food.

I am very averse to bringing myself forward in print, but as my account will only appear as an appendage to a former production, and as it will be confined to such topics as have connection with my authorship alone, I can hardly accuse myself of a personal intrusion.

Life is obstinate and clings closest where it is most hated.

A king is always a king - and a woman always a woman: his authority and her sex ever stand between them and rational converse.

My dreams were at once more fantastic and agreeable than my writings.

Elegance is inferior to virtue.

Teach him to think for himself? Oh, my God, teach him rather to think like other people!

It is hardly surprising that women concentrate on the way they look instead of what is in their minds since not much has been put in their minds to begin with.

What terrified me will terrify others; and I need only describe the spectre which had haunted my midnight pillow.

A slavish bondage to parents cramps every faculty of the mind.

James Joyce

James Augustine Aloysius Joyce was an Irish novelist, short story writer, poet and literary critic. He contributed to the modernist avant-garde movement and is regarded as one of the most influential and important writers of the 20th century. Born: February 2, 1882, Rathgar, Ireland. Died: January 13, 1941, Zürich, Switzerland.

Mistakes are the portals of discovery.

I've put in so many enigmas and puzzles that it will keep the professors busy for centuries arguing over what I meant, and that's the only way of insuring one's immortality.

Better pass boldly into that other world, in the full glory of some passion, than fade and wither dismally with age.

I am tomorrow, or some future day, what I establish today. I am today what I established yesterday or some previous day.

A man of genius makes no mistakes; his errors are volitional and are the portals of discovery.

There is no heresy or no philosophy which is so abhorrent to the church as a human being.

The actions of men are the best interpreters of their thoughts.

The artist, like the God of the creation, remains within or behind or beyond or above his handiwork, invisible, refined out of existence, indifferent, paring his fingernails.

A nation is the same people living in the same place.

When I die Dublin will be written in my heart.

Ireland is the old sow that eats her farrow.

Poetry, even when apparently most fantastic, is always a revolt against artifice, a revolt, in a sense, against actuality.

Think you're escaping and run into yourself. Longest way round is the shortest way home.

Christopher Columbus, as everyone knows, is honored by posterity because he was the last to discover America.

Your battles inspired me - not the obvious material battles but those that were fought and won behind your forehead.

Men are governed by lines of intellect - women: by curves of emotion.

The men that is now is only all palaver and what they can get out of you.

No pen, no ink, no table, no room, no time, no quiet, no inclination.

I fear those big words which make us so unhappy.

Whatever else is unsure in this stinking dunghill of a world a mother's love is not.

Shakespeare is the happy hunting ground of all minds that have lost their balance.

A corpse is meat gone bad. Well and what's cheese? Corpse of milk.

Irresponsibility is part of the pleasure of all art; it is the part the schools cannot recognize.

*Writing in English is the most ingenious
torture ever devised for sins committed in
previous lives. The English reading public
explains the reason why.*

Ireland sober is Ireland stiff.

*God spoke to you by so many voices but
you would not hear.*

Edgar Allan Poe

Edgar Allan Poe was an American writer, poet, editor, and literary critic. Poe is best known for his poetry and short stories, particularly his tales of mystery and the macabre. He is widely regarded as a central figure of Romanticism in the United States, and of American literature. Born: January 19, 1809, Boston, Massachusetts, United States. Died: October 7, 1849, Church Home & Hospital, Baltimore, Maryland, United States.

All religion, my friend, is simply evolved out of fraud, fear, greed, imagination, and poetry.

All that we see or seem is but a dream within a dream.

Beauty of whatever kind, in its supreme development, invariably excites the sensitive soul to tears.

Deep into that darkness peering, long I stood there, wondering, fearing, doubting, dreaming dreams no mortal ever dared to dream before.

Experience has shown, and a true philosophy will always show, that a vast, perhaps the larger portion of the truth arises from the seemingly irrelevant.

I have great faith in fools; self-confidence my friends call it.

I would define, in brief, the poetry of words as the rhythmical creation of Beauty.

It is by no means an irrational fancy that, in a future existence, we shall look upon what we think our present existence, as a dream.

It is the nature of truth in general, as of some ores in particular, to be richest when most superficial.

Science has not yet taught us if madness is or is not the sublimity of the intelligence.

The death of a beautiful woman, is unquestionably the most poetical topic in the world.

The ninety and nine are with dreams, content but the hope of the world made new, is the hundredth man who is grimly bent on making those dreams come true.

The nose of a mob is its imagination. By this, at any time, it can be quietly led.

They who dream by day are cognizant of many things which escape those who dream only by night.

To vilify a great man is the readiest way in which a little man can himself attain greatness.

We loved with a love that was more than love.

With me poetry has not been a purpose, but a passion.

Words have no power to impress the mind without the exquisite horror of their reality.

Oscar Wilde

Oscar Fingal O'Flahertie Wills Wilde was an Irish poet and playwright. After writing in different forms throughout the 1880s, he became one of the most popular playwrights in London in the early 1890s. Born: October 16, 1854, Westland Row, Dublin, Ireland. Died: November 30, 1900, Paris, France.

A dreamer is one who can only find his way by moonlight, and his punishment is that he sees the dawn before the rest of the world.

A little sincerity is a dangerous thing, and a great deal of it is absolutely fatal.

A poet can survive everything but a misprint.

A work of art is the unique result of a unique temperament.

All art is quite useless.

All bad poetry springs from genuine feeling.

Always forgive your enemies - nothing annoys them so much.

Ambition is the last refuge of the failure.

An excellent man; he has no enemies; and none of his friends like him.

Arguments are extremely vulgar, for everyone in good society holds exactly the same opinion.

Art is individualism, and individualism is a disturbing and disintegrating force.

Art is the most intense mode of individualism that the world has known.

Art should never try to be popular. The public should try to make itself artistic.

As long as war is regarded as wicked, it will always have its fascination. When it is looked upon as vulgar, it will cease to be popular.

Between men and women there is no friendship possible. There is passion, enmity, worship, love, but no friendship.

Biography lends to death a new terror.

Children begin by loving their parents; after a time they judge them; rarely, if ever, do they forgive them.

Death and vulgarity are the only two facts in the nineteenth century that one cannot explain away.

Deceiving others. That is what the world calls a romance.

Do you really think it is weakness that yields to temptation? I tell you that there are terrible temptations which it requires strength, strength and courage to yield to.

Education is an admirable thing, but it is well to remember from time to time that nothing that is worth knowing can be taught.

Everybody who is incapable of learning has taken to teaching.

Experience is one thing you can't get for nothing.

Experience is simply the name we give our mistakes.

He has no enemies, but is intensely disliked by his friends.

How can a woman be expected to be happy with a man who insists on treating her as if she were a perfectly normal human being.

How marriage ruins a man! It is as demoralizing as cigarettes, and far more expensive.

I can resist everything except temptation.

I choose my friends for their good looks, my acquaintances for their good characters, and my enemies for their intellects. A man cannot be too careful in the choice of his enemies.

I have the simplest tastes. I am always satisfied with the best.

I never travel without my diary. One should always have something sensational to read in the train.

I see when men love women. They give them but a little of their lives. But women when they love give everything.

I sometimes think that God in creating man somewhat overestimated his ability.

I suppose society is wonderfully delightful. To be in it is merely a bore. But to be out of it is simply a tragedy.

I think that God, in creating man, somewhat overestimated his ability.

I want my food dead. Not sick, not dying, dead.

If one could only teach the English how to talk, and the Irish how to listen, society here would be quite civilized.

If there was less sympathy in the world, there would be less trouble in the world.

If you are not too long, I will wait here for you all my life.

If you pretend to be good, the world takes you very seriously. If you pretend to be bad, it doesn't. Such is the astounding stupidity of optimism.

It is a very sad thing that nowadays there is so little useless information.

It is better to be beautiful than to be good. But... it is better to be good than to be ugly.

William Faulkner

William Cuthbert Faulkner was an American writer known for his novels and short stories set in the fictional Yoknapatawpha County, based on Lafayette County, Mississippi, where Faulkner spent most of his life. Born: September 25, 1897, New Albany, Mississippi, United States. Died: July 6, 1962, Byhalia, Mississippi, United States.

You cannot swim for new horizons until you have courage to lose sight of the shore.

Don't do what you can do - try what you can't do.

Unless you're ashamed of yourself now and then, you're not honest

Always dream and shoot higher than you know you can do. Don't bother just to be better than your contemporaries or predecessors. Try to be better than yourself.

If we Americans are to survive it will have to be because we choose and elect and defend to be first of all Americans; to present to the world one homogeneous and unbroken front, whether of white Americans or black ones or purple or blue or green... If we in America have reached that point in our desperate culture when we must murder children, no matter for what reason or what color, we don't deserve to survive, and probably won't.

Read, read, read. Read everything -- trash, classics, good and bad, and see how they do it. Just like a carpenter who works as an apprentice and studies the master. Read! You'll absorb it. Then write. If it's good, you'll find out. If it's not, throw it out of the window.

Be scared. You can't help that. But don't be afraid.

Don't bother just to be better than others. Try to be better than yourself.

Given the choice between the experience of pain and nothing, I would choose pain.

To understand the world, you must first understand a place like Mississippi.

Life is a process of preparing to be dead for a long time.

Gratitude is a quality similar to electricity: it must be produced and discharged and used up in order to exist at all.

You don't love because: you love despite; not for the virtues, but despite the faults.

Facts and truth really don't have much to do with each other.

We must be free not because we claim freedom, but because we practice it.

At one time I thought the most important thing was talent. I think now that the young man must possess or teach himself, training himself, in infinite patience, which is to try and to try until it comes right. He must train himself in ruthless intolerance- that is to throw away anything that is false no matter how much he might love that page or that paragraph. The most important thing is insight, that is to be-curiosity-to wonder, to mull, and to muse why it is that man does what he does, and if you have that, then I don't think the talent makes much difference, whether you've got it or not.

So, never be afraid. Never be afraid to raise your voice for honesty and truth and compassion, against injustice and lying and greed. If you, not just you in this room tonight, but in all the thousands of other rooms like this one about the world today and tomorrow and next week, will do this, not as a class or classes, but as individuals, men and women, you will change the earth.

Always dream and shoot higher than you know you can do.

To live anywhere in the world today and be against equality because of race or color is like living in Alaska and being against snow.

A gentleman accepts the responsibility of his actions and bears the burden of their consequences.

There is no such thing as bad whiskey. Some whiskeys just happen to be better than others. But a man shouldn't fool with booze until he's fifty; then he's a damn fool if he doesn't.

Our most treasured family heirloom are our sweet family memories. The past is never dead, it is not even past.

H. G. Wells

Herbert George Wells was an English writer. Prolific in many genres, he wrote dozens of novels, short stories, and works of social commentary, history, satire, biography and autobiography. His work also included two books on recreational war games. Born: September 21, 1866, Bromley High Street, London, United Kingdom. Died: August 13, 1946, The Regent's Park, London, United Kingdom.

Adapt or perish, now as ever, is nature's inexorable imperative.

Advertising is legalized lying.

Affliction comes to us, not to make us sad but sober; not to make us sorry but wise.

Beauty is in the heart of the beholder.

Crime and bad lives are the measure of a State's failure, all crime in the end is the crime of the community.

Cynicism is humor in ill health.

Every time I see an adult on a bicycle, I no longer despair for the future of the human race.

History is a race between education and catastrophe.

Human history becomes more and more a race between education and catastrophe.

Human history in essence is the history of ideas.

I must confess that my imagination refuses to see any sort of submarine doing anything but suffocating its crew and floundering at sea.

I want to go ahead of Father Time with a scythe of my own.

If we don't end war, war will end us.

If you fell down yesterday, stand up today.

In politics, strangely enough, the best way to play your cards is to lay them face upwards on the table.

Moral indignation is jealousy with a halo.

No passion in the world is equal to the passion to alter someone else's draft.

Nothing leads so straight to futility as literary ambitions without systematic knowledge.

The doctrine of the Kingdom of Heaven, which was the main teaching of Jesus, is certainly one of the most revolutionary doctrines that ever stirred and changed human thought.

The uglier a man's legs are, the better he plays golf - it's almost a law.

There's nothing wrong in suffering, if you suffer for a purpose. Our revolution didn't abolish danger or death. It simply made danger and death worthwhile.

Gabriel García Márquez

Gabriel José de la Concordia García Márquez was a Colombian novelist, short-story writer, screenwriter, and journalist, known affectionately as Gabo or Gabito throughout Latin America. Born: March 6, 1927, Aracataca, Colombia. Died: April 17, 2014, Mexico City, Mexico.

Ultimately, literature is nothing but carpentry. With both you are working with reality, a material just as hard as wood.

It always amuses me that the biggest praise for my work comes for the imagination, while the truth is that there's not a single line in all my work that does not have a basis in reality. The problem is that Caribbean reality resembles the wildest imagination.

A person doesn't die when he should but when he can.

No, not rich. I am a poor man with money, which is not the same thing.

Everything that goes into my mouth seems to make me fat, everything that comes out of my mouth embarrasses me.

If God hadn't rested on Sunday, He would have had time to finish the world.

The problem with marriage is that it ends every night after making love, and it must be rebuilt every morning before breakfast.

The truth is that I know very few novelists who have been satisfied with the adaptation of their books for the screen.

Injections are the best thing ever invented for feeding doctors.

From the moment I wrote 'Leaf Storm' I realized I wanted to be a writer and that nobody could stop me and that the only thing left for me to do was to try to be the best writer in the world.

Nobody deserves your tears, but whoever deserves them will not make you cry.

It is not true that people stop pursuing dreams because they grow old, they grow old because they stop pursuing dreams.

He who awaits much can expect little.

Fiction was invented the day Jonas arrived home and told his wife that he was three days late because he had been swallowed by a whale.

People spend a lifetime thinking about how they would really like to live. I asked my friends and no one seems to know very clearly. To me it's very clear now. I wish my life could have been like the years when I was writing 'Love in the Time of Cholera.'

She discovered with great delight that one does not love one's children just because they are one's children but because of the friendship formed while raising them.

Faulkner is a writer who has had much to do with my soul, but Hemingway is the one who had the most to do with my craft - not simply for his books, but for his astounding knowledge of the aspect of craftsmanship in the science of writing.

I must try and break through the cliches about Latin America. Superpowers and other outsiders have fought over us for centuries in ways that have nothing to do with our problems. In reality we are all alone.

The most important thing Paris gave me was a perspective on Latin America. It taught me the differences between Latin America and Europe and among the Latin American countries themselves through the Latins I met there.

I think that the idea that I'm writing for many more people than I ever imagined has created a certain general responsibility that is literary and political. There's even pride involved, in not wanting to fall short of what I did before.

What matters in life is not what happens to you but what you remember and how you remember it.

A man knows when he is growing old because he begins to look like his father.

Always remember that the most important thing in a good marriage is not happiness, but stability.

The interpretation of our reality through patterns not our own, serves only to make us ever more unknown, ever less free, ever more solitary.

I don't believe in God, but I'm afraid of Him.

In journalism just one fact that is false prejudices the entire work. In contrast, in fiction one single fact that is true gives legitimacy to the entire work. That's the only difference, and it lies in the commitment of the writer. A novelist can do anything he wants so long as he makes people believe in it.

Necessity has the face of a dog.

The heart's memory eliminates the bad and magnifies the good.

Fame is very agreeable, but the bad thing is that it goes on 24 hours a day.

Tricks you need to transform something which appears fantastic, unbelievable into something plausible, credible, those I learned from journalism. The key is to tell it straight. It is done by reporters and by country folk.

I don't know who said that novelists read the novels of others only to figure out how they are written. I believe it's true. We aren't satisfied with the secrets exposed on the surface of the page: we turn the book around to find the seams.

An early-rising man is a good spouse but a bad husband.

Mary McCarthy

Mary Therese McCarthy was an American novelist, critic and political activist, best known for her novel The Group, her marriage to critic Edmund Wilson, and her storied feud with playwright Lillian Hellman. Born: June 21, 1912, Seattle, Washington, United States. Died: October 25, 1989, Manhattan, New York, United States.

We all live in suspense from day to day; in other words, you are the hero of your own story.

We are the hero of our own story.

Every word she writes is a lie, including and and the.

You mustn't force sex to do the work of love or love to do the work of sex.

In violence, we forget who we are.

Liberty, as it is conceived by current opinion, has nothing inherent about it; it is a sort of gift or trust bestowed on the individual by the state pending good behavior.

I am putting real plums into an imaginary cake.

Every age has a keyhole to which its eye is pasted.

Europe is the unfinished negative of which America is the proof.

Being abroad makes you conscious of the whole imitative side of human behavior. The ape in man.

The immense popularity of American movies abroad demonstrates that Europe is the unfinished negative of which America is the proof.

Bureaucracy, the rule of no one, has become the modern form of despotism.

The American character looks always as if it had just had a rather bad haircut, which gives it, in our eyes at any rate, a greater humanity than the European, which even among its beggars has an all too professional air.

I'm afraid I'm not sufficiently inhibited about the things that other women are inhibited about for me. They feel that you've given away trade secrets.

People with bad consciences always fear the judgment of children.

The suspense of a novel is not only in the reader, but in the novelist, who is intensely curious about what will happen to the hero.

When an American heiress wants to buy a man, she at once crosses the Atlantic. The only really materialistic people I have ever met have been Europeans.

Is it really so difficult to tell a good action from a bad one? I think one usually knows right away or a moment afterward, in a horrid flash of regret.

The labor of keeping house is labor in its most naked state, for labor is toil that never finishes, toil that has to be begun again the moment it is completed, toil that is destroyed and consumed by the life process.

The theater is the only branch of art much cared for by people of wealth; like canasta, it does away with the brother of talk after dinner.

Life for the European is a career; for the American it is a hazard.

In science, all facts, no matter how trivial or banal, enjoy democratic equality.

If someone tells you he is going to make a 'realistic decision', you immediately understand that he has resolved to do something bad.

In politics, it seems, retreat is honorable if dictated by military considerations and shameful if even suggested for ethical reasons.

Labor is work that leaves no trace behind it when it is finished, or if it does, as in the case of the tilled field, this product of human activity requires still more labor, incessant, tireless labor, to maintain its identity as a 'work' of man.

I suppose everyone continues to be interested in the quest for the self, but what you feel when you're older, I think, is that you really must make the self.

Robert Louis Stevenson

Robert Louis Stevenson was a Scottish novelist, essayist, poet and travel writer. He is best known for works such as Treasure Island, Strange Case of Dr Jekyll and Mr. Hyde, Kidnapped and A Child's Garden of Verses. Born: November 13, 1850, Edinburgh, United Kingdom. Died: December 3, 1894, Vailima, Apia, Samoa.

A friend is a gift you give yourself.

Absences are a good influence in love and keep it bright and delicate.

All human beings are commingled out of good and evil.

An aim in life is the only fortune worth finding.

Compromise is the best and cheapest lawyer.

Don't judge each day by the harvest you reap but by the seeds that you plant.

Every heart that has beat strongly and cheerfully has left a hopeful impulse behind it in the world and bettered the tradition of mankind.

Every man has a sane spot somewhere.

For my part, I travel not to go anywhere, but to go. I travel for travel's sake. The great affair is to move.

Give us grace and strength to forbear and to persevere. Give us courage and gaiety and the quiet mind, spare to us our friends, soften to us our enemies.

I never weary of great churches. It is my favorite kind of mountain scenery. Mankind was never so happily inspired as when it made a cathedral.

I travel not to go anywhere, but to go. I travel for travel's sake. The great affair is to move.

If a man loves the labour of his trade, apart from any question of success or fame, the gods have called him.

In marriage, a man becomes slack and selfish, and undergoes a fatty degeneration of his moral being.

It is a golden maxim to cultivate the garden for the nose, and the eyes will take care of themselves.

It is better to lose health like a spendthrift than to waste it like a miser.

It is the mark of a good action that it appears inevitable in retrospect.

Keep your eyes open to your mercies. The man who forgets to be thankful has fallen asleep in life.

Keep your fears to yourself, but share your courage with others.

Life is not a matter of holding good cards, but of playing a poor hand well.

Man is a creature who lives not upon bread alone, but primarily by catchwords.

Marriage is like life - it is a field of battle, not a bed of roses.

Marriage is one long conversation, chequered by disputes.

Marriage: A friendship recognized by the police.

Nothing like a little judicious levity.

Our business in life is not to succeed, but to continue to fail in good spirits.

Politics is perhaps the only profession for which no preparation is thought necessary.

That man is a success who has lived well, laughed often and loved much.

The price we have to pay for money is sometimes liberty.

There is only one difference between a long life and a good dinner: that, in the dinner, the sweets come last.

J. R. R. Tolkien

john Ronald Reuel Tolkien was an English writer, poet, philologist, and academic, best known as the author of the high fantasy works The Hobbit and The Lord of the Rings. Born: January 3, 1892, Bloemfontein, South Africa. Died: September 2, 1973, Bournemouth, United Kingdom

*All that is gold does not glitter, not all
those who wander are lost; the old that is
strong does not wither, deep roots are not
reached by the frost.*

Not all those who wander are lost.

*All we have to decide is what to do with
the time that is given us.*

Still round the corner there may wait, A new road or a secret gate.

Courage is found in unlikely places.

If more of us valued food and cheer and song above hoarded gold, it would be a merrier world.

Faithless is he that says farewell when the road darkens.

It's the job that's never started as takes longest to finish.

Many that live deserve death. And some that die deserve life. Can you give it to them? Then do not be too eager to deal out death in judgement. For even the very wise cannot see all ends.

The wide world is all about you: you can fence yourselves in, but you cannot forever fence it out.

Short cuts make long delays.

You have been chosen, and you must therefore use such strength and heart and wits as you have.

The proper study of Man is anything but Man; and the most improper job of any man, even saints (who at any rate were at least unwilling to take it on), is bossing other men. Not one in a million is fit for it, and least of all those who seek the opportunity.

I don't know half of you half as well as I should like; and I like less than half of you half as well as you deserve.

Do not meddle in the affairs of Wizards, for they are subtle and quick to anger.

A box without hinges, key, or lid, yet golden treasure inside is hid.

Hobbits are an unobtrusive but very ancient people, more numerous formerly than they are today; for they love peace and quiet and good tilled earth: a well-ordered and well-farmed countryside was their favorite haunt.

So comes snow after fire, and even dragons have their ending!

It does not do to leave a live dragon out of your calculations, if you live near him.

They say it is the first step that costs the effort. I do not find it so. I am sure I could write unlimited 'first chapters'. I have indeed written many.

Go not to the Elves for counsel, for they will say both no and yes.

A pen is to me as a beak is to a hen.

A safe fairyland is untrue to all worlds.

It may be the part of a friend to rebuke a friend's folly.

I should like to save the Shire, if I could - though there have been times when I thought the inhabitants too stupid and dull for words, and have felt that an earthquake or an invasion of dragons might be good for them.

Myth and fairy-story must, as all art, reflect and contain in solution elements of moral and religious truth (or error), but not explicit, not in the known form of the primary 'real' world.

George Bernard Shaw

George Bernard Shaw, known at his insistence simply as Bernard Shaw, was an Irish playwright, critic, polemicist and political activist. His influence on Western theatre, culture and politics extended from the 1880s to his death and beyond. Born: July 26, 1856, Portobello, Dublin, Ireland. Died: November 2, 1950, Ayot Saint Lawrence, United Kingdom.

A fool's brain digests philosophy into folly, science into superstition, and art into pedantry. Hence University education.

A government that robs Peter to pay Paul can always depend on the support of Paul.

A happy family is but an earlier heaven.

A life spent making mistakes is not only more honorable, but more useful than a life spent doing nothing.

A little learning is a dangerous thing, but we must take that risk because a little is as much as our biggest heads can hold.

Animals are my friends... and I don't eat my friends.

Baseball has the great advantage over cricket of being sooner ended.

Beauty is a short-lived tyranny.

Beware of false knowledge; it is more dangerous than ignorance.

Beware of the man who does not return your blow: he neither forgives you nor allows you to forgive yourself.

Caesar was a man of great common sense and good taste, meaning thereby a man without originality or moral courage.

Clever and attractive women do not want to vote; they are willing to let men govern as long as they govern men.

Creation is a miracle of daily recurrence. 'A miracle a minute' would not be a bad slogan for God.

Democracy substitutes election by the incompetent many for appointment by the corrupt few.

Do not waste your time on Social Questions. What is the matter with the poor is Poverty; what is the matter with the rich is Uselessness.

Every man over forty is a scoundrel.

Everything happens to everybody sooner or later if there is time enough.

Except during the nine months before he draws his first breath, no man manages his affairs as well as a tree does.

First love is only a little foolishness and a lot of curiosity.

Give a man health and a course to steer, and he'll never stop to trouble about whether he's happy or not.

Hegel was right when he said that we learn from history that man can never learn anything from history.

Hell is full of musical amateurs.

Home life is no more natural to us than a cage is natural to a cockatoo.

I dislike feeling at home when I am abroad.

I learned long ago, never to wrestle with a pig. You get dirty, and besides, the pig likes it.

I never thought much of the courage of a lion tamer. Inside the cage he is at least safe from people.

I often quote myself. It adds spice to my conversation.

I would like to take you seriously, but to do so would be an affront to your intelligence.

If all the economists were laid end to end, they'd never reach a conclusion.

If history repeats itself, and the unexpected always happens, how incapable must Man be of learning from experience.

If I were a woman, I'd simply refuse to speak to any man or do anything for men until I'd got the vote.

If you cannot get rid of the family skeleton, you may as well make it dance.

I'm an atheist and I thank God for it.

Imagination is the beginning of creation. You imagine what you desire, you will what you imagine and at last you create what you will.

In a battle all you need to make you fight is a little hot blood and the knowledge that it's more dangerous to lose than to win.

Independence? That's middle class blasphemy. We are all dependent on one another, every soul of us on earth.

It is the mark of a truly intelligent person to be moved by statistics.

Just do what must be done. This may not be happiness, but it is greatness.

Lack of money is the root of all evil.

Liberty means responsibility. That is why most men dread it.

Life does not cease to be funny when people die any more than it ceases to be serious when people laugh.

Life isn't about finding yourself. Life is about creating yourself.

Life levels all men. Death reveals the eminent.

Love is a gross exaggeration of the difference between one person and everybody else.

Marriage is an alliance entered into by a man who can't sleep with the window shut, and a woman who can't sleep with the window open.

Marriage is good enough for the lower classes: they have facilities for desertion that are denied to us.

Marriage is popular because it combines the maximum of temptation with the maximum of opportunity.

Martyrdom: The only way a man can become famous without ability.

Men are wise in proportion, not to their experience, but to their capacity for experience.

My reputation grows with every failure.

Never fret for an only son, the idea of failure will never occur to him.

No man ever believes that the Bible means what it says: He is always convinced that it says what he means.

One man that has a mind and knows it can always beat ten men who haven't and don't.

Only on paper has humanity yet achieved glory, beauty, truth, knowledge, virtue, and abiding love.

Parentage is a very important profession, but no test of fitness for it is ever imposed in the interest of the children.

Patriotism is your conviction that this country is superior to all others because you were born in it.

Peace is not only better than war, but infinitely more arduous.

Famous Philosophers

These philosophers are a bonus track. You can check more in our recently publication Classic Inspirational quotes from famous Philosophers.

Aristotle

Aristotle was a Greek philosopher and polymath during the Classical period in Ancient Greece. Taught by Plato, he was the founder of the Lyceum, the Peripatetic school of philosophy, and the Aristotelian tradition. Born: 384 BC, Stagira, Greece Died: 322 BC, Chalcis, Greece

---

A friend to all is a friend to none.

A great city is not to be confounded with a populous one.

All human actions have one or more of these seven causes: chance, nature, compulsions, habit, reason, passion, desire.

All men by nature desire knowledge.

At his best, man is the noblest of all animals; separated from law and justice he is the worst.

Bashfulness is an ornament to youth, but a reproach to old age.

Change in all things is sweet.

Courage is a mean with regard to fear and confidence.

Courage is the first of human qualities because it is the quality which guarantees the others.

Education is an ornament in prosperity and a refuge in adversity.

Education is the best provision for old age.

Arthur Schopenhauer

Arthur Schopenhauer was a German philosopher. He is best known for his 1818 work The World as Will and Representation, which characterizes the phenomenal world as the product of a blind and insatiable noumenal will. Born: February 22, 1788, Gdańsk, Poland Died: September 21, 1860, Free City of Frankfurt

---

After your death you will be what you were before your birth.

Almost all of our sorrows spring out of our relations with other people.

Change alone is eternal, perpetual, immortal.

Every parting gives a foretaste of death, every reunion a hint of the resurrection.

Friends and acquaintances are the surest passport to fortune.

Great men are like eagles, and build their nest on some lofty solitude.

Hatred is an affair of the heart; contempt that of the head.

I've never known any trouble than an hour's reading didn't assuage.

Just remember, once you're over the hill you begin to pick up speed.

Martyrdom is the only way a man can become famous without ability.

Baruch Spinoza

Baruch Spinoza was a Dutch philosopher of Portuguese Sephardi origin. One of the early thinkers of the Enlightenment and modern biblical criticism, including modern conceptions of the self and the universe, he came to be considered one of the great rationalists of 17th-century philosophy. Born: November 24, 1632, Amsterdam, Netherlands. Died: February 21, 1677, The Hague, Netherlands.

All happiness or unhappiness solely depends upon the quality of the object to which we are attached by love.

Ambition is the immoderate desire for power.

Do not weep; do not wax indignant. Understand.

Freedom is absolutely necessary for the progress in science and the liberal arts.

God is the indwelling and not the transient cause of all things.

Happiness is a virtue, not its reward.

I do not know how to teach philosophy without becoming a disturber of established religion.

Men govern nothing with more difficulty than their tongues, and can moderate their desires more than their words.

Peace is not an absence of war, it is a virtue, a state of mind, a disposition for benevolence, confidence, justice.

Peace is not the absence of war, but a virtue based on strength of character.

Buddha

The Buddha was a philosopher, mendicant, meditator, spiritual teacher, and religious leader who lived in ancient India. Born: Lumbini, Nepal. Died: Kushinagar, India

---

Better than a thousand hollow words, is one word that brings peace.

Do not dwell in the past, do not dream of the future, concentrate the mind on the present moment.

Do not overrate what you have received, nor envy others. He who envies others does not obtain peace of mind.

Even death is not to be feared by one who has lived wisely.

Hatred does not cease by hatred, but only by love; this is the eternal rule.

He who loves 50 people has 50 woes; he who loves no one has no woes.

Health is the greatest gift, contentment the greatest wealth, faithfulness the best relationship.

It is better to travel well than to arrive.

Just as a candle cannot burn without fire, men cannot live without a spiritual life.

No one saves us but ourselves. No one can and no one may. We ourselves must walk the path.

David Hume

David Hume was a Scottish Enlightenment philosopher, historian, economist, librarian and essayist, who is best known today for his highly influential system of philosophical empiricism, skepticism, and naturalism. Born: May 7, 1711, Edinburgh, United Kingdom. Died: August 25, 1776, Edinburgh, United Kingdom

A purpose, an intention, a design, strikes everywhere even the careless, the most stupid thinker.

Beauty in things exists in the mind which contemplates them.

Beauty, whether moral or natural, is felt, more properly than perceived.

Generally speaking, the errors in religion are dangerous; those in philosophy only ridiculous.

Human Nature is the only science of man; and yet has been hitherto the most neglected.

Scholastic learning and polemical divinity retarded the growth of all true knowledge.

The corruption of the best things gives rise to the worst.

The heights of popularity and patriotism are still the beaten road to power and tyranny.

Epictetus

Epictetus was a Greek Stoic philosopher. He was born a slave at Hierapolis, Phrygia and lived in Rome until his banishment, when he went to Nicopolis in northwestern Greece for the rest of his life. His teachings were written down and published by his pupil Arrian in his Discourses and Enchiridion. Born: 50 AD, Hierapolis, Turkey. Died: 135 AD, Nicopolis, Greece

All religions must be tolerated... for every man must get to heaven in his own way.

First learn the meaning of what you say, and then speak.

Freedom is not procured by a full enjoyment of what is desired, but by controlling the desire.

Freedom is the right to live as we wish.

If you wish to be a writer, write.

Is freedom anything else than the right to live as we wish? Nothing else.

It is not death or pain that is to be dreaded, but the fear of pain or death.

It is the nature of the wise to resist pleasures, but the foolish to be a slave to them.

Friedrich Nietzsche

Friedrich Nietzsche was a German philosopher, cultural critic, composer, poet, writer, and philologist whose work has exerted a profound influence on modern intellectual history. Born: October 15, 1844, Röcken, Lützen, Germany. Died: August 25, 1900, Weimar, Germany

---

A casual stroll through the lunatic asylum shows that faith does not prove anything.

A pair of powerful spectacles has sometimes sufficed to cure a person in love.

A subject for a great poet would be God's boredom after the seventh day of creation.

All truly great thoughts are conceived by walking.

An artist has no home in Europe except in Paris.

Art is the proper task of life. Art raises its head where creeds relax.

Experience, as a desire for experience, does not come off. We must not study ourselves while having an experience.

Faith: not wanting to know what is true.

Jean-Jacques Rousseau

Jean-Jacques Rousseau was a Genevan philosopher, writer, and composer. His political philosophy influenced the progress of the Enlightenment throughout Europe, as well as aspects of the French Revolution and the development of modern political, economic and educational thought. Born: June 28, 1712, Geneva, Switzerland. Died: July 2, 1778, Ermenonville, France.

A feeble body weakens the mind.

Absolute silence leads to sadness. It is the image of death.

Although modesty is natural to man, it is not natural to children. Modesty only begins with the knowledge of evil.

Base souls have no faith in great individuals.

Free people, remember this maxim: we may acquire liberty, but it is never recovered if it is once lost.

Gratitude is a duty which ought to be paid, but which none have a right to expect.

Happiness: a good bank account, a good cook, and a good digestion.

Nature never deceives us; it is we who deceive ourselves.

No man has any natural authority over his fellow men.

O love, if I regret the age when one savors you, it is not for the hour of pleasure, but for the one that follows it.

John Locke

John Locke was an English philosopher and physician, widely regarded as one of the most influential of Enlightenment thinkers and commonly known as the "Father of Liberalism". Born: August 29, 1632, Wrington, United Kingdom. Died: October 28, 1704, High Laver, United Kingdom

All mankind... being all equal and independent, no one ought to harm another in his life, health, liberty or possessions.

All men are liable to error; and most men are, in many points, by passion or interest, under temptation to it.

As people are walking all the time, in the same spot, a path appears.

Education begins the gentleman, but reading, good company and reflection must finish him.

Fortitude is the guard and support of the other virtues.

Government has no other end, but the preservation of property.

I have always thought the actions of men the best interpreters of their thoughts.

No man's knowledge here can go beyond his experience.

Reading furnishes the mind only with materials of knowledge; it is thinking that makes what we read ours.

Reverie is when ideas float in our mind without reflection or regard of the understanding.

Laozi

Lao Tzu, also rendered as Laozi and Lao-Tze, was an ancient Chinese philosopher and writer. He is the reputed author of the Tao Te Ching, the founder of philosophical Taoism, and a deity in religious Taoism and traditional Chinese religions.

A good traveler has no fixed plans and is not intent on arriving.

A man with outward courage dares to die; a man with inner courage dares to live.

Act without expectation.

Being deeply loved by someone gives you strength, while loving someone deeply gives you courage.

Care about what other people think and you will always be their prisoner.

Do you have the patience to wait until your mud settles and the water is clear?

Kindness in words creates confidence.
Kindness in thinking creates profoundness.
Kindness in giving creates love.

Music in the soul can be heard by the universe.

Nature does not hurry, yet everything is accomplished.

Respond intelligently even to unintelligent treatment

We hope this collection Inspire You
Humblepics.com

Printed in Great Britain
by Amazon

30871832R00128